BARBECUE

BARBECUE

Annie Nichols

hamlyn

First published in Great Britain in 1997
by Hamlyn, a division of Octopus Publishing Group Ltd
2–4 Heron Quays, London E14 4JP

This edition published 2002 by Octopus Publishing Group Ltd

Reprinted 2004

Copyright ©1997, 2002 Octopus Publishing Group Ltd

ISBN 0 600 61117 5

Printed in China

NOTES

Both metric and imperial measurements have been given in all
recipes. Use one set of measurements only and not a
mixture of both.

Standard level spoon measurements are used in all recipes.
1 tablespoon = one 15 ml spoon
1 teaspoon = one 5 ml spoon

Eggs should be medium to large unless otherwise stated.
The Department of Health advises that eggs should not be
consumed raw. This book contains dishes made with raw or
lightly cooked eggs. It is prudent for more vulnerable people such
as pregnant and nursing mothers, invalids, the elderly, babies and
young children to avoid uncooked or lightly cooked dishes made
with eggs. Once prepared, these dishes should be kept
refrigerated and used promptly.

Milk should be full fat unless otherwise stated.

Meat and poultry should be cooked thoroughly. To test if poultry
is cooked, pierce the flesh through the thickest part with a
skewer or fork – the juices should run clear, never pink or red.
Do not re-freeze poultry that has been frozen previously and
thawed. Do not re-freeze a dish that has been frozen previously.

Pepper should be freshly ground black pepper unless
otherwise stated.

Fresh herbs should be used, unless otherwise stated. If unavailable,
use dried herbs as an alternative but halve the quantities stated.

Measurements for canned food have been given as a standard
metric equivalent.

Nuts and nut derivatives
This book includes dishes made with nuts and nut derivatives. It
is advisable for customers with known allergic reactions to nuts
and nut derivatives and those who may be potentially vulnerable
to these allergies, such as pregnant and nursing mothers, invalids,
the elderly, babies and children, to avoid dishes made with nuts
and nut oils. It is also prudent to check the labels of pre-prepared
ingredients for the possible inclusion of nut derivatives.

Vegetarians should look for the 'V' symbol on a cheese to ensure
it is made with vegetarian rennet. There are vegetarian forms of
Parmesan, Feta, Cheddar, Cheshire, Red Leicester, dolcelatte
and many goats' cheeses, among others.

Ovens should be preheated to the specified temperature – if
using a fan-assisted oven, follow the manufacturer's instructions
for adjusting the time and the temperature.

Cooking times are approximate. They have been estimated using
a charcoal-fired barbecue and will vary according to the size and
type of the grill, weather conditions and the intensity of heat.
How far food is from the fire and the amount of food on the grill
will also affect the overall cooking times.

Before using wooden skewers or string, soak them in water for 30
minutes to avoid burning.

Contents

Introduction

Given the slightest hint of summer, a strange phenomenon occurs. Men who aren't normally trusted in the kitchen are seen wearing aprons and paper chef's hats and sallying forth, tongs in hand, to rule the barbecue!

Barbecuing is fun, and food always seems to taste better cooked outdoors. There is nothing more delicious than succulent juicy food with a golden crunchy char-grilled crust, hot from the grill. Even with our unpredictable summers, barbecuing has become increasingly popular in recent years. It's a healthy, exciting way of cooking and the choice of accompaniments, marinades and sauces can make it as simple or as spectacular as you like.

Cooking over charcoal is, in fact, an easy cooking method. Given good preparation and planning, it should be relaxed and enjoyable. Just follow a few simple rules and you'll have time to spend with your guests or – even better – get them to take part! Throw a brunch barbecue. Serve Buck's Fizz and brioche topped with smoked salmon and soured cream. Prepare delicious Flip-top Oysters and Mussels – raw oysters and mussels in their shells, placed on the hot grill. They will open within minutes – just

flip off the shells and serve with melted butter, wedges of lime and lemon and Champagne to wash it all down.

Plan a barbecue for a crisp autumn day after a long vigorous walk to work up an appetite. Serve mulled wine and nuts toasted on the grill while you wait for game birds or venison to cook. Even on a chilly winter's day, wrap up warmly and hold a barbecue. Serve hot soup while the barbecue is heating and throw on some quick-cooking food to feed the ravenous.

You will find scores of suggestions in this book for different marinades, sauces and accompaniments. That is just what they are, suggestions – so try your own experiments with some different combinations and have fun!

CHOOSING A BARBECUE

With the vast range of barbecues now on the market, the choice can seem very confusing. This need not be the case; you should just identify a few important points that are crucial to your needs. Decide how often you are likely to use the barbecue and whether this warrants a large state-of-the-art machine. Do you often entertain on a large scale or just for your family or a few friends? Perhaps you like to set off for a spontaneous picnic, where a small portable barbecue would be the most suitable. These are the most important considerations when you come to choose your barbecue.

GAS BARBECUES

The main advantage of gas barbecues is that the heat is instant and usually easy to control. As long as you have enough gas on hand, you won't have to worry about refuelling a dying fire. A disadvantage is that they can't provide that delicious char-grilled flavour that you get with charcoal or wood.

THE KETTLE GRILL

This covered grill with a hinged lid is useful in windy weather, when the hood acts as a windbreak. When the lid is closed it acts like an oven; the food is surrounded by heat reflected by the hood so the cooking process is much faster and you can cook large joints of meat. Aromatics such as herbs or wood chips will give delicious flavour to food cooked in this way. The main disadvantage is that the grid is not usually adjustable and you therefore cannot regulate the cooking temperature very easily.

THE BRAZIER

These portable, open grills are usually free-standing with wheels or detachable legs, though there are sophisticated models with hoods and wind shields. Choose a sturdy model with strong legs set at a convenient height – they are often set rather low and this can be back-breaking if you're tall.

Look for one with air vents that can be easily opened and closed, and an adjustable grill rack with two or three variable heights, allowing you to vary the distance from the heat.

Other refinements include electric, battery or hand-powered rôtisseries for spit-roasting. Again, it is important to choose a model where the spit can be adjusted to different heights.

HIBACHI

The Japanese word *hibachi* means 'fire box'. This cast-iron grill is one of the most popular barbecues because it is small, inexpensive and, though heavy, easily transportable and thus ideal for camping and picnics. Small versions are perfect for cooking a barbecue *à deux* though there are also larger sizes.

BUILT-IN PERMANENT BARBECUES

Build your barbecue on a site a little away from the house (to avoid smoke-filled rooms) and protected from prevailing winds. Line the inside with fire bricks, place a metal container on the base to hold the fuel and a grate underneath for ventilation and to catch the ashes. Set metal pegs, nails or bricks poking out at different heights to allow the cooking grid to be adjusted. Complete packs are now available from DIY stores and garden centres with everything you'll need to build your own barbecue.

THE IMPROVISED BARBECUE

Given a little inspiration and a few tools you can improvise the simplest of barbecues either indoors in the hearth of your fireplace (but don't use charcoal indoors as this can be very dangerous), or outdoors by setting a metal grid over some bricks.

OTHER BARBECUES

There are many other types of barbecue available, including little cast-iron and terracotta pots, and even disposable barbecues which last for about an hour or so, and are fine for an impromptu barbecue when you're away from home, or if you are cooking just a few small items.

FUELS

If you have an electric or gas-fired barbecue, you do not need to worry about the benefits of charcoal versus wood, though you will find that aromatics will give extra flavour to your food.

CHARCOAL

There is a good deal of debate about which fuel is the best to use for cooking on the barbecue. Charcoal is certainly the most common and my preference is for lumpwood charcoal or good-quality briquettes (though not the ones with chemical fluids added) because they give a good, uniform, intense heat.

WOOD

Hardwood gives off a very pleasant aroma, and you could choose from grapevine, cherry, apple, olive, ash, oak and many more. You should avoid resinous softwoods. However, wood barbecues need constant supervision to achieve continuous heat. So, unless you are lucky enough to have a reliable supply of hardwood, you will be much more likely to cook with charcoal.

AROMATICS

When added to your fire, aromatics will give off a very pleasant aroma and impart a little of their flavour to the food – a joint cooked in a kettle grill with hickory smoke is absolutely delicious. Packs of wood chips are now available from most DIY stores, garden centres and even from some large supermarkets. It is not absolutely essential, either, to pre-soak wood chips as they can be scattered straight on to the coals. However, if you soak them for 1–2 hours before cooking they will last longer and give a stronger, more smoky flavour.

Place the wood chips on a sheet of aluminium foil or a metal tray and set

PREPARING BUTTERRFLY PRAWNS

1 Remove the heads. Cut along the back from the thickest part towards the tail.

2 Open out the prawn and remove the dark vein running down its back. Press out gently to form the butterfly shape.

3 After marinating, thread the prawns on to pre-soaked wooden skewers, then grill on the barbecue for 5–6 minutes, turning once.

this directly on the coals beneath the food. A tin can be placed upside down over the food to give an even more intense smoky flavour.

Try adding a bunch of woody herbs to the fire, a little at a time. The aromas of dried fennel stalks, sage, rosemary, thyme or juniper are just wonderful. Dried herbs will burn very quickly and so are better added towards the end of cooking.

LIGHTING A BARBECUE

Line the base of your barbecue with heavy-duty foil. This will reflect the heat and also make it easier to clean up afterwards. First spread wood or charcoal 2.5–5 cm/1–2 inches deep over the base to check you have enough. Pile the fuel into a pyramid shape and push a fire-lighter into the centre or, alternatively, place dry kindling and crumpled paper under the coals. Light with a match and leave to burn. After 30–40 minutes, when the flames have subsided and the charcoal is covered in a fine white ash, rake the coals evenly over the base; you are then ready to cook. Do not be tempted to begin cooking before this, or while there are any flames – you will just burn and blacken the food on the outside, leaving it raw on the inside.

COOKING ON A BARBECUE

To top up the barbecue as you cook, place extra coals around the outside to warm up, and then gradually rake them into the fire, a few at a time, as they start to burn. If you add cold charcoal to the fire it will lower the heat. To control the intensity of the heat, push the coals apart for a lower heat or pile them together for a more intense one. Adjust the height of the grill rack; sear food close to the coals, then raise the rack to finish cooking. It is also possible to vary the heat by starting the food over the hottest part of the fire then moving it to a cooler area. Opening and closing the vents on your barbecue, if you have them, will also help to control the heat.

Cooking times are approximate. They have been estimated using a charcoal-fired barbecue and will vary greatly according to the size and type of grill, different weather conditions and the intensity of the heat. The distance of the food from the fire and the amount of food on the grill will also affect the overall cooking times.

EQUIPMENT

Although not absolutely essential, the following items will make for easier barbecuing.

LONG-HANDLED TONGS

Useful for turning food and putting it on and taking it off the grill. Use a separate pair for the coals.

LONG-PRONGED FORK

Don't pierce food while it is cooking; this will remove precious juices and flavours and dry out the food. Use only towards the end of cooking to check if meat or poultry is cooked.

SKEWERS

For brochettes and kebabs – soak wooden skewers for 30 minutes before use to prevent burning.

DRIP TRAY

Heavy-duty foil or a metal freezer tray can be placed on the coals under the food to catch the juices for basting or for use in the finished sauce. It also prevents flare-ups from dripping fat.

BASTING BRUSH

For basting food and oiling the grill.

HINGED BASKETS

These are great for turning whole fish or any fragile items with ease.

LONG MATCHES

Extra-long matches make fire-lighting easier and safer.

OVEN GLOVE, CLOTH OR APRON

To protect you and your clothes.

RUBBER GLOVES

For handling black and messy coals when setting up the fire.

CHOPPING BOARD AND KNIFE

Keep handy for cutting up food.

ALUMINIUM FOIL

To wrap food before cooking and to keep it warm.

BARBECUE TIPS

1 Make sure you have ample fuel.

2 Keep charcoal dry, as it won't burn well when damp.

3 Allow enough time to start the fire properly and for the embers to form.

4 Do not put salt in marinades for meat as this draws out the juices and dries out the meat. Season just before or just after cooking.

5 Always oil the barbecue grill well to prevent the food sticking.

6 Keep food in the refrigerator before use and bring it to room temperature just before cooking.

7 Cut food to an even size so it will cook evenly. Place longer-cooking foods on the barbecue first, then add any quick-cooking items.

8 Remember that food continues to cook after you remove it from the heat.

9 Sugary glazes should be brushed on just before the end of cooking – they will probably burn if added earlier.

10 Be well prepared and keep everything you will need to hand.

11 Lean meat has a tendency to dry out, so bard it with extra fat or wrap it in bacon before barbecuing.

12 Never use petrol, paraffin or other flammable liquids when lighting your fire. Be safe!

COOKING IN BANANA LEAVES

1 Dip the leaves in boiling water, then drain and place the filling at one end

2 Fold one corner of the leaf over the filling, then the other. Repeat to form a neat triangular parcel.

3 Tie a loop of string around one corner of the triangle, then the other. If you can't find banana leaves, use foil instead.

Fish and Seafood

Spiedini of Prawns in a Balsamic Marinade

12 large butterflied raw king prawns in their shells
5 tablespoons olive oil
2 tablespoons balsamic vinegar
2 tablespoons chopped fresh oregano or marjoram
2 garlic cloves, crushed
pepper

1 To prepare the prawns, remove the legs and cut off the heads with a small sharp knife. Holding a prawn with the back uppermost, slice along its length, from the thickest part towards the tail, cutting almost but not quite through it. Carefully remove the dark vein that runs down its back. Gently press the prawn to flatten it out and make a butterfly shape. Repeat with the remaining prawns and rinse well under running water. Pat the prawns dry on kitchen paper and place them in a large shallow dish.

2 Mix together the oil, vinegar, oregano or marjoram, garlic and pepper and pour over the prawns, turning to coat them well. Cover and leave to marinate for 1 hour. If using wooden skewers, soak them in cold water for 30 minutes.

3 Remove the prawns from the marinade, reserving any marinade. Thread 3 prawns on to each of 4 skewers.

4 Cook the prawns on a well oiled barbecue over moderately hot coals for 3–4 minutes, turning them once and basting with any remaining marinade, until the flesh is opaque and just cooked. Serve at once.

Serves 4
Preparation time: 20 minutes, plus marinating
Cooking time: 3–4 minutes

Stuffed Baby Squid

Perfect for the barbecue, these sweet tasting baby squid are filled with a Mediterranean-inspired stuffing. Make sure you do not over-fill them or they may split open during cooking.

- 500 g/1 lb baby squid, cleaned and prepared
- 50 g/2 oz black olives, pitted and chopped
- 2 tablespoons bottled capers, drained and chopped
- 1–2 garlic cloves, crushed
- 4 tomatoes, skinned, deseeded and chopped
- 4 tablespoons chopped fresh oregano
- 125 g/4 oz fresh white breadcrumbs
- 1½ tablespoons lemon juice
- 4 tablespoons olive oil, plus extra for brushing

1 Chop the squid tentacles finely and place them in a bowl. Add the olives, capers, garlic, tomatoes, oregano, breadcrumbs, lemon juice and 4 tablespoons olive oil. Mix well.
2 Use this mixture to stuff the squid. Secure the open end of each one with a cocktail stick, soaked in water for 20 minutes. Brush the squid lightly with oil.
3 Cook the stuffed squid on an oiled barbecue grill over moderately hot coals for about 3–4 minutes, turning frequently, until just cooked. Serve immediately.

Serves 4
Preparation time: 40 minutes
Cooking time: 3–4 minutes

VARIATION

Baby Squid with Chilli and Coriander Stuffing

- 500 g/1 lb baby squid, cleaned and prepared
- 3 spring onions, thinly sliced
- 2 garlic cloves, crushed
- 1–2 red chillies, deseeded and chopped
- 2 tablespoons chopped fresh coriander
- 1 lime
- 175 g/6 oz ground almonds
- 2 tablespoons groundnut oil

To make the stuffing, chop the squid tentacles finely, as described in the main recipe, place them in a bowl and add the spring onions, garlic, chillies and fresh coriander. Grate the lime rind finely, then squeeze out the juice. Add the rind to the mixture, mix well and moisten with 1 tablespoon of the juice. Stir in the almonds and oil. Proceed as in the main recipe.

Mussels and Clams Marinière with Orange

- 750 g/1½ lb mussels, scrubbed well and beards removed
- 750 g/1½ lb clams, scrubbed well
- 2 bay leaves
- 2 sprigs of thyme
- 2 shallots, finely chopped
- 1 garlic clove, finely chopped
- 25 g/1 oz butter, melted
- ½ teaspoon lightly crushed peppercorns
- juice and finely grated rind of 2 oranges
- 200 ml/7 fl oz dry white wine
- 2 tablespoons chopped fresh parsley

1 Place two large double pieces of heavy duty foil on a work surface and bring up the edges of the foil slightly. On one piece of foil place the mussels and on the other piece place the clams. Add 1 bay leaf and 1 sprig of thyme to each parcel.

2 Mix together all the remaining ingredients except the parsley and divide between the two parcels. Bring the edges of the parcels together and press together to seal.

3 Place the parcels on the barbecue grill and leave to cook for 5–10 minutes, shaking occasionally. When cooked all the mussels and clams will be opened (discard any that have not). Tip the mussels and clams immediately into a large colander set over a bowl and strain the resulting juices through a muslin lined sieve.

4 Serve the mussels immediately with the strained cooking liquor poured over them and sprinkled with the chopped parsley.

Serves 4
Preparation time: 30 minutes
Cooking time: 5–10 minutes

Salmon and Samphire en Papilotte

Samphire – or sea asparagus as it is also known – is a delicious coastal plant which grows on salt marshes. Here it is combined with rich salmon and a nutty pistachio and basil butter in a foil parcel. Hasselback potatoes make a perfect accompaniment.

- 4 salmon fillets, about 200 g/7 oz each
- 125–175 g/4–6 oz samphire

PISTACHIO AND BASIL BUTTER:
- 125 g/4 oz butter, slightly softened
- 50 g/2 oz unpeeled, unsalted pistachio nuts
- 2 tablespoons chopped fresh basil
- 1 garlic clove, crushed
- 1–2 teaspoons freshly squeezed lime juice
- salt and pepper

HASSELBACK POTATOES:
- 16 small new potatoes
- 3 tablespoons olive oil
- sea salt flakes

1 To make the pistachio and basil butter, place the butter, pistachios, basil, garlic and lime juice in a food processor or blender. Add salt and pepper to taste and blend until the sauce is smooth and green. Spoon the mixture into a small bowl, cover and chill in the refrigerator.
2 Place each salmon fillet on a double piece of foil large enough to enclose it completely. Top each fillet with a quarter of the samphire and add a generous tablespoon of the pistachio butter. Bring up the edges of the foil and press together to seal each parcel.
3 Divide the potatoes among 4 skewers. Using a small sharp knife, make thin slashes across each potato, then brush all the potatoes with the olive oil and sprinkle with some sea salt flakes.
4 Cook the potato skewers on an oiled, preheated barbecue grill over hot coals for 20–25 minutes, adding the salmon parcels for the final 15–20 minutes. Just before serving, carefully open one of the foil parcels and check that the fish is cooked through. It should flake easily when tested with the point of a knife, but still be moist. Serve the parcels on individual plates, with the Hasselback potatoes.

Serves 4
Preparation time: 10 minutes
Cooking time: 20–25 minutes

VARIATION

Ginger and Mint Butter

Use this fragrant gingery butter in place of the pistachio and basil butter.

- 125 g/4 oz butter, slightly softened
- 1 tablespoon grated fresh root ginger
- 2 tablespoons chopped fresh mint
- salt and pepper

Beat all the ingredients together in a bowl. Continue as in the main recipe.

Polenta-crusted Fish with Lemon and Sesame Mayonnaise

- 4 x 175 g/6 oz boneless firm white fish fillets such as John Dory, cod or sole
- 50 g/2 oz polenta
- 2 tablespoons olive oil
- salt and pepper

LEMON AND SESAME MAYONNAISE:

- 1 egg yolk
- 2 tablespoons fresh lemon juice
- ½ teaspoon Dijon mustard
- 150 ml/5 fl oz sunflower oil
- 1 teaspoon sesame oil
- finely grated rind of 1 small lemon

1 First make the mayonnaise. Place the egg yolk, lemon juice and mustard in a food processor and process until amalgamated. Mix the sunflower and sesame oil together and, with the motor running, gradually add the oils in a slow thin stream. When the mayonnaise is thick stir in the lemon rind and season to taste. Transfer to a bowl, cover and set aside.

2 Brush the fish fillets all over with the olive oil. Lay the fillets on a plate flesh side up and sprinkle liberally with the polenta. Season with salt and pepper.

3 Heat a metal griddle on the barbecue and when hot enough oil well. (Alternatively lay a piece of heavy duty foil on the barbecue grill and continue as above.) Lay the fish fillets on the griddle flesh side down and cook for 3 minutes on each side until just cooked. Serve the fillets immediately with a crisp salad and the lemon and sesame mayonnaise.

Serves 4
Preparation time: 15 minutes
Cooking time: 6 minutes

Cod in a Nutty Coating with a Banana Coconut Salsa

- 75 g/3 oz unsalted roasted peanuts, finely chopped
- ¼ teaspoon chilli powder
- 6 allspice berries, finely crushed
- ½ teaspoon salt
- 75 g/3 oz butter, melted
- 4 x 175–250 g/6–8 oz cod fillets

BANANA AND COCONUT SALSA:

- 75 g/3 oz grated fresh coconut or 25 g/1 oz unsweetened desiccated coconut
- 1 small garlic clove, crushed
- finely grated rind and juice of 1 lime
- ½ small red onion, finely chopped
- 2 tablespoons chopped fresh coriander
- 3 bananas
- salt and pepper

1 Mix together the ground peanuts, chilli powder, crushed allspice and salt and sprinkle on to a large plate. Dip each cod fillet into the melted butter and then into the peanut mixture, shaking off any excess. Cover and set aside.

2 If using desiccated coconut, place in a bowl with warm water to cover. Leave to soak for 20 minutes, then strain through a sieve, pressing the coconut against the sides with the back of a spoon to squeeze out any excess moisture.

3 To make the banana salsa, mix together the crushed garlic, lime rind and juice, red onion, coriander and coconut. Just before serving, chop the banana into small dice and gently stir into the salsa mixture.

4 Heat a metal griddle on the barbecue and when hot enough oil well. Place the cod fillets on the griddle and cook for 4–6 minutes until just done, turning once. Serve immediately with the banana and coconut salsa.

Serves 4
Preparation time: 20 minutes, plus soaking, if using desiccated coconut
Cooking time: 4–6 minutes

Whole Baked Fish in Banana Leaves

Measure the thickness of the fish, then cook it for 10 minutes per 2.5 cm/1 inch. Banana leaves can be bought at ethnic markets.

- 1 whole fish, about 1.25–1.5 kg/2½–3 lb (e.g. parrot fish, snapper or red sea bream), cleaned and scaled, with 2–3 diagonal slits cut in each side
- 1 tablespoon freshly squeezed lime juice mixed with 1 teaspoon salt
- 1 small onion, roughly chopped
- 1 red or yellow pepper, cored, deseeded and roughly chopped
- 2.5 cm/1 inch piece of fresh root ginger, peeled and roughly chopped
- 2 garlic cloves, roughly chopped
- 2 fresh red chillies, deseeded and roughly chopped
- 1 stick of lemon grass, chopped
- 125 ml/4 fl oz coconut milk
- ½ teaspoon chilli powder
- 15 g/½ oz fresh coriander
- banana leaves or foil, for wrapping

1 Rub the slits in the fish with the lime juice and salt and set it aside.

2 Place all the remaining ingredients except the wrapping into a food processor or blender and purée until smooth. Scrape the paste into a bowl.

3 Dip the banana leaves into boiling water and drain. Place the fish on top. Rub in a quarter of the paste, turn the fish over and rub in another quarter of the mixture. Wrap the leaves securely around the fish, making sure there are no holes, and tie with string, or wrap in a double thickness of foil.

4 Place the wrapped fish on a barbecue grill over moderately hot coals and cook for 10–15 minutes on each side, until the flesh is tender. Transfer the parcel to a large platter and turn back the leaves or foil to reveal the fish.

5 Heat the remaining spice paste in a small pan and serve with the fish.

Serves 4
Preparation time: 20 minutes
Cooking time: 20–30 minutes

Swordfish with Black Olive Butter

- 4 x 175 g/6 oz swordfish steaks
- 2 tablespoons olive oil

BLACK OLIVE BUTTER:

- 125 g/4 oz unsalted butter, softened
- 25 g/1oz pitted black olives, very finely chopped

- ½ teaspoon anchovy paste
- 1 garlic clove, crushed
- 1 tablespoon capers, finely chopped
- juice and finely grated rind of ½ lemon
- salt and pepper

1 To make the black olive butter, place the butter in a bowl and add the olives, anchovy paste, garlic, capers and lemon juice and rind. Beat until well combined and season to taste. Alternatively mix in a food processor.

2 Place a piece of parchment or greaseproof paper on a work surface and spread the butter down the middle. Roll the paper over and twist the ends until you have a neat sausage. Chill in the refrigerator until firm.

3 Brush the swordfish steaks with the olive oil, place on an oiled preheated barbecue grill and grill for 3–4 minutes on each side until just cooked. Unroll the black olive butter and cut it into slices. Serve each steak with a slice of butter.

Serves 4
Preparation time: 15 minutes, plus chilling
Cooking time: 6–8 minutes

Sea Bass with Lime Aïoli

- 4 large potatoes, unpeeled
- 4 tablespoons olive oil
- 4 x 175–250 g/6–8 oz sea bass fillets
- salt and pepper

LIME AIOLI:

- 4–6 garlic cloves, crushed
- 2 egg yolks
- juice and finely grated rind of 2 limes
- 300 ml/½ pint extra virgin olive oil

1 First make the aïoli. Place the garlic and egg yolks in a food processor or blender, add the lime juice and process briefly to mix. With the machine running, gradually add the olive oil in a thin steady stream until the mixture forms a thick cream. Turn into a bowl, stir in the lime rind and season to taste. Set aside.

2 Slice the potatoes thinly and brush well with olive oil. Sprinkle the slices with salt and pepper and place on a barbecue grill and cook for 2–3 minutes on each side or until tender and golden. Remove from the heat and keep warm while you cook the fish.

3 Score the sea bass fillets, brush well with the remaining olive oil and place on the barbecue grill, skin side down. Cook for 3–4 minutes until just cooked, turning once. Remove from the heat and serve with the potatoes and the aïoli.

Serves 4

Preparation time: 30 minutes
Cooking time: 3–4 minutes

2 Strain the oil through a sieve lined with muslin or a clean tea towel. Pour into a sterilized jar or bottle.

3 Brush the sardines with a little of the chilli oil, sprinkle with coarse sea salt and cook on an oiled barbecue grill over hot coals for 6–8 minutes or until just cooked, turning once. Serve immediately, with lemon wedges, crusty bread and a tomato and onion salad, if liked.

Serves 4

Preparation time: 15 minutes, plus infusing

Cooking time: 6–8 minutes

VARIATION

Grilled Sardines with Herb Oil

- 2 garlic cloves, crushed
- 6 tablespoons olive oil
- 1 tablespoon chopped fresh oregano
- 1 tablespoon chopped fresh thyme
- 1 tablespoon chopped fresh parsley
- 1 tablespoon lemon juice
- 1 teaspoon fennel seeds, crushed
- 12 small sardines, cleaned and scaled
- coarse sea salt and pepper

Mix the garlic, oil, herbs, lemon juice and fennel seeds together.

Brush the sardines well with this mixture sprinkle with a little sea salt and black pepper and cook as described in the main recipe.

Grilled Sardines with Chilli Oil

Homemade chilli oil – less potent than the commercial product – gives the sardines a slight zing without blowing the roof of your mouth off! If you are using the commercial variety instead, mix just a few drops with the 125 ml/4 fl oz of olive oil.

- 125 ml/4 fl oz olive oil
- 2 tablespoons chopped dried red chillies
- 12 small sardines, cleaned and scaled
- coarse sea salt

1 Place the oil and chillies in a small saucepan and heat very gently for about 10 minutes. Remove from the heat, cover and leave to cool and infuse for 8–12 hours or overnight.

Tuna with Anchovies and Caper Vinaigrette

- **4 x 250 g/8 oz thick tuna steaks**
- **12 anchovies in oil, drained and cut in half**
- **4 garlic cloves, cut into thin slivers**
- **2 tablespoons olive oil**
- **salt and pepper**

CAPER VINAIGRETTE:
- **100 ml/3½ fl oz extra virgin olive oil**
- **2 tablespoons white wine vinegar**
- **1 teaspoon Dijon mustard**
- **1 tablespoon chopped fresh tarragon**
- **1 tablespoon chopped fresh flat leaf parsley**
- **2 tablespoons capers, rinsed and crushed**
- **pinch of sugar**

1 To make the caper vinaigrette, whisk together the olive oil, vinegar and mustard in a small bowl. Stir in the tarragon, parsley and capers and season with salt, pepper and a pinch of sugar. Cover and set aside.

2 With a small sharp knife, make 6 small incisions in each tuna steak. Using the end of the knife poke a piece of anchovy fillet and a sliver of garlic into each incision.

3 Brush all the steaks with olive oil and season with salt and pepper. Place the steaks on the barbecue grill and cook for 3–4 minutes on each side until just cooked. Serve with the caper vinaigrette and a crisp green salad.

Serves 4
Preparation time: 15 minutes
Cooking time: 6-8 minutes

Seared Peppered Tuna

Some people are allergic to pink peppercorns, so you may wish to use crushed black or white peppercorns instead.

- 250 g/8 oz rice noodles
- 1½ tablespoons sesame oil
- 1½ tablespoons sesame seeds, toasted, plus 1 tablespoon, to garnish (optional)
- 2 tablespoons freshly squeezed lime juice
- 5 tablespoons groundnut oil
- 2 garlic cloves, crushed
- 4 x 175 g/6 oz tuna steaks, skinned

- 4 tablespoons dried pink peppercorns, crushed
- salt

PICKLED GINGER:
- 6 tablespoons rice vinegar
- 1 tablespoon sugar
- 1 teaspoon salt
- 50 g/2 oz piece of fresh root ginger, peeled and cut into wafer-thin slices

1 To prepare the pickled ginger, place the vinegar, sugar and salt in a small pan. Bring to the boil, add the ginger, lower the heat and simmer for about 1–2 minutes. Remove from the heat, transfer to a bowl and leave to cool.

2 Prepare the noodles according to the packet instructions. Drain and refresh under cold water, then drain again. Tip into a bowl, add the sesame oil and sesame seeds and toss lightly.

3 Combine the lime juice, groundnut oil, garlic and salt to taste in a shallow dish, large enough to hold all the tuna in a single layer. Add the fish, toss lightly until coated, cover the dish and marinate the tuna for 1 hour, turning once.

4 Put the peppercorns on a plate. Drain the tuna, discarding the marinade. Coat the edges of the steaks with the peppercorns. Sprinkle with salt.

5 Cook on an oiled grill over moderately hot coals for 1 minute on each side to sear the edges. Slice thinly and serve with the ginger and noodles, sprinkled with sesame seeds, if liked.

Serves 4

Preparation time: 20 minutes, plus marinating
Cooking time: 2 minutes

Stuffed Rainbow Trout with Soured Cream and Horseradish Sauce

Pretty, gleaming, iridescent trout are delicious when served with a simple lemony stuffing and a creamy horseradish sauce.

- 150 g/5 oz butter
- 125 g/4 oz blanched almonds, toasted and chopped
- 125 g/4 oz fresh white breadcrumbs
- juice and finely grated rind of 1 lemon
- 4 x 375 g/12 oz rainbow trout, cleaned
- salt and pepper

HORSERADISH SAUCE:

- 125 ml/4 fl oz soured cream
- 4 teaspoons grated horseradish
- 4 tablespoons chopped fresh parsley
- 2 tablespoons chopped fresh mint

1 To make the horseradish sauce, place the soured cream, horseradish, parsley and mint in a food processor or blender. Blend until smooth, then turn into a bowl and season to taste.
2 Melt 125 g/4 oz of the butter in a small saucepan, add the chopped almonds, breadcrumbs, lemon rind and juice, and salt and pepper. Mix well, stuff into the trout cavities, then reshape the fish.
3 Brush 4 large double pieces of foil with the remaining butter, lay a trout on each and wrap up tightly. Cook on a preheated grill over moderately hot coals for 20–25 minutes, or until the fish comes away from the bone, turning once. Serve immediately with the sauce and new potatoes cooked on the barbecue.

Serves 4
Preparation time: 20 minutes
Cooking time: 20–25 minutes

Spicy Fish Satay

- 500 g/1 lb mackerel fillets
- 1 garlic clove, crushed
- 2.5 cm/1 inch piece of fresh root ginger, chopped and crushed in a garlic press
- 2 teaspoons light soy sauce
- 1 tablespoon lime or lemon juice
- 1 small red chilli, very finely chopped
- ½ papaya, peeled, deseeded and cut into chunks

SATAY SAUCE:

- 2 tablespoons sunflower or groundnut oil
- 1 large garlic clove, crushed
- 1 shallot, finely chopped
- 400 ml/14 fl oz water
- 1 tablespoon dark brown sugar
- ½ teaspoon chilli powder
- 125 g/4 oz unsalted roasted peanuts, finely ground
- 1 tablespoon lime or lemon juice
- salt and pepper

1 Cut each mackerel fillet into 2.5 cm/1 inch diagonal strips and place in a bowl. Mix together the garlic, ginger, soy sauce, lime or lemon juice and chilli and pour over the mackerel pieces in the bowl. Turn to coat well, cover and leave to marinate for 30 minutes–1 hour.

2 To make the satay sauce, heat the oil in a small saucepan. Add the garlic and shallot and cook for 3–4 minutes until lightly golden. Pour in the water, sugar, chilli powder and peanuts, stir well and bring to a boil, reduce the heat and simmer, stirring occasionally, for 10–15 minutes or until the sauce has thickened. Remove from the heat and stir in the lime or lemon juice and season with salt and pepper.

3 Remove the fish from the marinade and thread 3 pieces on to each skewer adding a piece of papaya to the end of each one.

4 Place the skewers on an oiled preheated barbecue grill and cook for 3–4 minutes on each side. Serve with the warm satay sauce.

Serves 4

Preparation time: 30 minutes, plus marinating
Cooking time: 20–25 minutes

Meat Dishes

Tamarind Spareribs with Mint Relish

1 kg/2 lb meaty pork spareribs

MARINADE:

1 teaspoon mustard seeds

3 tablespoons tamarind paste or 2 tablespoons lime or lemon juice

2 garlic cloves, crushed

1 tablespoon light soy sauce

6 tablespoons honey

1 teaspoon ground cumin

1 teaspoon ground coriander

½ teaspoon chilli powder

yogurt, to serve

MINT RELISH:

50 g/2 oz chopped fresh mint

½ small red onion, very finely chopped

1 small green chilli, seeded and chopped

2 tablespoons lemon juice

1 teaspoon sugar

salt and pepper

1 To make the marinade, place the mustard seeds in a dry frying pan and cook over low heat until the seeds start to pop. Remove the pan from the heat and leave the seeds to cool, then crush them lightly.

2 Mix the remaining marinade ingredients with the crushed mustard seeds. Place the spareribs in a large shallow dish and pour over the marinade. Turn the spareribs to coat, then cover and leave to marinate for 1–2 hours.

3 To make the mint relish, place the mint, onion, chilli, lemon juice and sugar in a food processor or blender. Work until smooth, pushing down with a spatula occasionally. Turn out into a bowl and season to taste with salt and pepper.

4 Remove the spareribs from the marinade and place on an oiled barbecue grill and cook for about 15–20 minutes, turning frequently. Serve with the relish and yogurt.

Serves 4

Preparation time: 15 minutes, plus marinating

Cooking time: 15–20 minutes

Prosciutto and Pear Sticks

- **2 ripe pears**
- **6 slices prosciutto**

TO SERVE:

- **salad leaves**
- **shavings of Pecorino or Parmesan**
- **cracked black pepper**
- **extra virgin olive oil**

1 Cut each slice of prosciutto in half lengthways. Cut each pear into 6 wedges and remove the core.

2 Wrap a piece of prosciutto around each pear wedge and thread 3 wedges on to each skewer.

3 Place the skewers on an oiled barbecue grill and cook for 2–3 minutes on each side. Serve at once on a bed of salad leaves. Using a vegetable peeler, shave the cheese over the skewers, sprinkle with cracked black pepper and drizzle with a little olive oil.

Serves 4
Preparation time: 10 minutes
Cooking time: 4–6 minutes

Pork and Juniper Kebabs and Ruby Grapefruit Salsa

- 500 g/1 lb pork fillet, trimmed and cut into 4 cm/1½ inch cubes
- 16 bay leaves
- 2 tablespoons chopped fresh chives
- 2 tablespoons very finely chopped red onion

MARINADE:

- 3 ruby red grapefruit
- 2 tablespoons lime juice
- 3 tablespoons honey
- 2 garlic cloves, crushed
- 6 juniper berries, finely crushed
- 100 ml/3½ fl oz walnut or olive oil
- pepper

1 To make the marinade, squeeze the juice from one of the grapefruit. Peel and segment the remaining grapefruit, working over a bowl so that no juice is wasted.

2 To make the grapefruit salsa, chop the grapefruit segments and place them in a bowl, stir in the chives and onion, season and set aside.

3 Stir the remaining marinade ingredients into the bowl of juice and mix well. Add the pork cubes, turn to coat thoroughly, then cover and leave to marinate for 1–2 hours.

4 Remove the meat from the marinade and thread on to 4 skewers, placing a bay leaf between each piece of meat.

5 Place the kebabs on an oiled barbecue grill and cook for 15–20 minutes, turning and basting frequently with the remaining marinade. Serve with the grapefruit salsa.

Serves 4
Preparation time: 15 minutes, plus 1–2 hours marinating
Cooking time: 15–20 minutes

Kofta Kebabs

This speciality from the Middle East consists of spiced minced lamb or beef pressed around skewers, grilled and served with a minty yogurt dip. If using wooden skewers, soak them in cold water for about 30 minutes before use.

- 500 g/1 lb minced lamb or beef
- 1 onion, grated
- 50 g/2 oz pine nuts, roasted and chopped
- 1 tablespoon chopped fresh oregano
- ½ teaspoon ground cumin
- ½ teaspoon ground coriander
- salt and pepper

YOGURT DIP:

- 375 g/12 oz Greek yogurt
- 3 tomatoes, skinned, deseeded and chopped
- 1 tablespoon chopped fresh mint
- pinch of cayenne pepper
- salt

1 To make the yogurt dip, mix the yogurt, chopped tomatoes and mint in a bowl. Season with a pinch each of cayenne pepper and salt. Cover the bowl and chill in the refrigerator until required.
2 Place the minced lamb or beef in a food processor and grind to a smooth paste. Alternatively, pass through the finest blade of a mincer. Scrape into a bowl and stir in the onion, pine nuts, oregano, cumin and coriander. Season with salt and pepper.
3 Mould the mixture around 4 long skewers forming it either into sausage shapes or balls. Place on a well oiled barbecue grill over hot coals and cook for about 10–12 minutes until the meat is browned all over and cooked through.
4 Remove the kebabs from the skewers, if liked, or serve one skewer per person, together with the yogurt dip. Pitta bread and a crisp salad of cos lettuce are suitable accompaniments.

Serves 4
Preparation time: 20 minutes
Cooking time: 10–12 minutes

VARIATION

Fresh Cucumber Relish

Try this refreshing relish as an alternative to the yogurt dip.

1 Peel ½ a cucumber, cut it in half and remove the seeds, using a teaspoon. Cut the flesh into fine dice and place in a bowl. Add 3 finely sliced spring onions, 2 tablespoons chopped fresh mint, 1 tablespoon red wine vinegar and the grated rind and juice of ½ orange. Mix well, add salt and pepper to taste, then cover the bowl and refrigerate until required.

Shish Kebabs

- 1–2 garlic cloves, crushed
- 2 onions, grated
- juice and finely grated rind of 1 lemon
- 75 ml/3 fl oz olive oil
- 2 teaspoons bottled green peppercorns, drained and crushed
- 2 tablespoons chopped fresh oregano or parsley
- 500 g/1 lb piece of steak (e.g. sirloin, rump or fillet), cut into 2.5 cm/1 inch cubes
- 1 yellow pepper, cored, deseeded and cut into 2.5 cm/1 inch squares
- salt

1 Combine the garlic, grated onions, lemon juice and rind, olive oil, peppercorns and oregano or parsley in a large bowl. Mix well. Add the beef cubes and toss to coat. Cover the bowl and leave to marinate for 2–3 hours.

2 Using a slotted spoon, remove the beef cubes from the marinade. Thread the beef on to 4 long skewers, alternating with squares of the yellow pepper. Pour the remaining marinade into a jug.

3 Place the kebabs on an oiled barbecue grill over hot coals and cook for 3–4 minutes on each side, basting frequently with the remaining marinade.

Serve with grilled aubergines and couscous, bulgur wheat or rice.

Serves 4
Preparation time: 10 minutes, plus marinating
Cooking time: 6–8 minutes

Beef Kebabs with Beetroot and Horseradish Salsa

- 750 g/1½ lb piece sirloin steak, trimmed and cut into 16 long thin strips
- 8 long sprigs of rosemary
- 4 tablespoons balsamic vinegar
- 175 ml/6 fl oz red wine
- 4 tablespoons olive oil
- 1 tablespoon cracked black pepper
- salt

HORSERADISH SALSA:

- 250 g/8 oz cooked beetroot, peeled and chopped
- ½ red onion, finely chopped
- 1–2 tablespoons finely grated fresh horseradish or horseradish relish, or to taste

1 Thread 2 pieces of steak on to each sprig of rosemary concertina fashion and place in a shallow dish. Mix together the vinegar, wine, olive oil and pepper and pour over the steak. Turn to coat thoroughly, then cover and leave to marinate for 1–2 hours.

2 To make the horseradish salsa, mix the beetroot, onion and horseradish, season and set aside.

3 Remove the kebabs from the marinade, sprinkle with a little salt and place on an oiled barbecue grill and cook for 3–4 minutes on each side, basting frequently with the remaining marinade. Serve with the salsa.

Serves 4

Preparation time: 10 minutes, plus marinating

Cooking time: 6–8 minutes

Lamb Noisettes with Mint Pesto or Aubergine and Olive Paste

Two delicious pastes, both perfect with hot, freshly grilled lamb.

- **8 lamb noisettes**
- **2 tablespoons olive oil**

AUBERGINE AND OLIVE PASTE:

- **1 large aubergine, about 250 g/8 oz**
- **125 g/4 oz pitted black olives**
- **25 g/1 oz fresh parsley**
- **1 tablespoon coarse grain mustard**
- **2 garlic cloves, crushed**
- **salt and pepper**

MINT PESTO:

- **25 g/1 oz fresh mint**
- **15 g/½ oz fresh flat leaf parsley**
- **25 g/1 oz pistachio nuts, shelled**
- **2 garlic cloves**
- **125 ml/4 fl oz olive oil**
- **25 g/1 oz Parmesan cheese, grated**

1 To make the aubergine and olive paste, place the whole aubergine under a preheated grill for about 20 minutes, turning occasionally, until the skin is well charred and the flesh softened. Cool slightly, slit the skin and squeeze the aubergine over the sink to remove the bitter juices. Cut in half and scoop the flesh into a food processor or blender. Add the olives, parsley, mustard, garlic and salt and pepper. Purée until smooth, then spoon into a bowl and set aside.

2 To make the mint pesto, place the mint, parsley, pistachios and garlic in a food processor or blender and process until finely chopped. With the motor running, gradually add the olive oil in a thin steady stream until amalgamated. Pour the pesto into a bowl, stir in the Parmesan and add salt and pepper to taste.

3 Brush the noisettes with olive oil, sprinkle with pepper and cook on an oiled barbecue grill over hot coals for 4–5 minutes on each side.

4 Place on individual plates, spoon over the pesto or paste and serve. Grilled courgettes and their flowers are suitable accompaniments.

Serves 4
Preparation time: 30 minutes
Cooking time: 8–10 minutes

Lamb Loin Chops with Coriander Chutney

- 4 lamb loin chops
- 1 red onion, cut into 8 wedges

MARINADE:

- 2 garlic cloves, crushed
- 2.5 cm/1 inch piece of fresh root ginger, crushed in a garlic press
- 2 tablespoons sunflower or vegetable oil
- 2 teaspoons ground coriander
- 1 teaspoon ground cumin
- ½ teaspoon ground cloves
- ¼ teaspoon ground cinnamon
- ¼ teaspoon pepper
- ½ teaspoon salt

CORIANDER CHUTNEY:

- 8 tablespoons chopped fresh coriander
- 1 small green chilli, deseeded and finely chopped
- 1 teaspoon garam masala
- 1 teaspoon sugar
- 1 teaspoon salt
- 2 tablespoons lime or lemon juice

1 To make the marinade, mix together all the ingredients, except the salt, and place in a shallow dish. Rub the chops with the marinade, cover and leave to marinate for 2–3 hours, turning from time to time.

2 To make the coriander chutney, place all the ingredients in a food processor or blender and blend until smooth. Stop the machine every so often and push down any bits with a spatula and blend again. Turn into a small bowl to serve.

3 Place each lamb chop on a skewer. Pull the onion wedges apart and thread a few pieces on to the skewer with the chop.

4 Season the skewers with a little salt, place on an oiled barbecue and cook for 4–5 minutes on each side. Serve with the chutney and a green salad.

Serves 4
Preparation time: 5 minutes, plus marinating
Cooking time: 8–10 minutes

Butterflied Leg of Lamb with Flageolet Beans

- 250 g/8 oz dried flageolet beans or haricot beans
- 2 bay leaves
- 1 leg of lamb, boned and butterflied
- 3 tablespoons olive oil
- 4 whole bulbs of garlic
- 25 g/1 oz butter
- 1 large onion, finely chopped
- 6 celery sticks, cut into 1 cm/½ inch pieces
- 25 g/1 oz fresh mint or parsley, finely chopped
- salt and pepper

1 Place the beans in a bowl with cold water to cover. Soak overnight, then drain, rinse and drain again. Tip the beans into a large saucepan, add the bay leaves and cover with cold water. Bring to the boil, then boil rapidly for about 10 minutes, lower the heat and simmer gently for 50–60 minutes until just tender. Drain the beans well, discarding the bay leaves. Set aside.

2 Remove the skin and fat from the lamb, leaving only a thin layer. Brush with the oil and place flat on an oiled barbecue grill over hot coals. Sear for 5–6 minutes on each side, then turn and cook for 10–15 minutes more on each side. About 8–10 minutes before the end of the cooking time, wrap each garlic bulb in a double thickness of foil and place in the embers of the fire to soften the flesh.

3 When the meat is cooked, transfer it to a platter, cover with a tent of foil and leave to rest for 10 minutes. Meanwhile, melt the butter in a large saucepan. Add the onion and celery and cook gently for 10–12 minutes until softened but not coloured. Add the beans and heat through, stirring occasionally. Remove from the heat and toss with the mint or parsley.

4 Slice the lamb and serve with the flageolet beans. Add a bulb of roasted garlic to each portion and offer plenty of crusty bread.

Serves 6
Preparation time: 1¼ hours, plus soaking
Cooking time: 40–50 minutes

Rosemary Potatoes

This is a delicious potato recipe to serve with fish, poultry or meat – especially lamb, which goes so well with rosemary.

- 500 g/1 lb new potatoes, boiled in their skins for 10 minutes
- 4 long sprigs of rosemary
- 1 tablespoon olive oil
- 1 tablespoon sea salt flakes

1 Thread the potatoes on to the sprigs of rosemary, brush them with olive oil and sprinkle with sea salt.

2 Place on an oiled barbecue grill and cook for 10 minutes, turning occasionally.

Veal Escalopes with Artichoke Paste

These neat little veal parcels are filled with a sweet artichoke and tomato paste, enclosing a soft, molten ball of mozzarella. Bocconcini – tiny mozzarella cheeses – are available from delicatessens and supermarkets, or you could substitute a whole mozzarella cut into four. Ask your butcher to pound the veal escalopes very thinly, or do this yourself, placing each escalope between two sheets of polythene and pounding lightly with a rolling pin, taking care not to make any holes.

- 125 g/4 oz drained bottled artichokes in oil, 1 tablespoon oil reserved
- 4 sun-dried tomato halves in oil, drained
- 4 veal escalopes, about 125 g/4 oz each, pounded until thin
- 2 slices of prosciutto, cut in half
- 4 bocconcini or 1 mozzarella
- salt and pepper
- oil, for brushing

1 Place the artichokes, the reserved oil and sun-dried tomatoes in a food processor or blender and work to a smooth paste. Scrape into a bowl and stir in salt and pepper to taste.
2 Spread each escalope with a quarter of the artichoke paste, top with a half slice of prosciutto and a bocconcini. Fold the veal over to make a neat parcel and seal each end with a presoaked cocktail stick.

3 Brush the parcels with oil. Cook on an oiled grill over hot coals for about 4–5 minutes turning frequently.

Serves 4
Preparation time: 15–20 minutes
Cooking time: 4–5 minutes

Peppered Steak with Roasted Tomato and Garlic Sauce

- 4 x 175 g/6 oz fillet steaks
- 2 tablespoons mixed peppercorns, well crushed
- 3 tablespoons olive oil

TOMATO AND GARLIC SAUCE:

- 1 kg/2 lb ripe tomatoes, preferably plum
- 3 tablespoons extra virgin olive oil
- 8 whole garlic cloves, unpeeled
- 1 teaspoon sea salt
- 2 teaspoons caster sugar

1 To make the tomato and garlic sauce, cut the tomatoes in half lengthways and scoop out the seeds with a spoon. Lightly grease a baking sheet with a little of the olive oil and lay the tomatoes on top, cut side up, with the garlic cloves. Drizzle with the remaining olive oil.

2 Sprinkle the salt and sugar evenly over the tomatoes and place in a preheated oven, 180°C (350°F) Gas Mark 4, for 45–50 minutes. Remove the garlic cloves after 15 minutes or when the flesh is very soft. When cool enough to handle, pop the garlic flesh out of their skins and set aside.

3 Place the tomatoes, with any juices that have accumulated, and the garlic flesh in a food processor or blender and work until smooth. Strain through a sieve into a clean pan, season to taste and reheat when ready to serve.

4 To prepare the steaks, mix together the crushed peppercorns and olive oil on a plate. Dip each steak into the peppercorn oil and coat evenly on each side. Place the steaks on an oiled barbecue grill and cook for 2–3 minutes on each side for rare, up to 3–4 minutes on each side for medium rare, 4–5 minutes on each side for medium and 10–12 minutes on each side for well done.

5 Serve the steaks with the tomato and garlic sauce.

Serves 4
Preparation time: 30 minutes
Cooking time: 45–50 minutes for the tomatoes, plus:
4–6 minutes for rare steaks
6–8 minutes for medium rare
8–10 minutes for medium
10–12 minutes for well done
Oven temperature: 180°C (350°F) Gas Mark 4

Homemade Sausages with Mustard Aïoli

If you place the mincer attachments in the freezer for 30 minutes before use, the meat will come away more easily and the mincer will be easier to clean.

- sausage casings
- 500 g/1 lb lean shoulder pork
- 175 g/6 oz back fat without rind
- 1½ tablespoons coarse sea salt
- 4 tablespoons fresh thyme leaves
- ½ teaspoon ground bay
- pepper

MUSTARD AIOLI:
- 4–6 garlic cloves, crushed
- 2 egg yolks
- juice of ½ lemon, plus extra to taste
- 300 ml/½ pint extra virgin olive oil
- 2 tablespoons coarse grain mustard
- salt and pepper

1 Soak the sausage casings in cold water for 20 minutes, untangle any knots, then rinse thoroughly by pulling one end of the casing over the end of the tap and running cold water through it.
2 Trim any skin or gristle from the shoulder and back fat and cut into pieces. Pass the meat through the medium blade of a mincer or, alternatively, finely chop it by hand.
3 Place the meat in a large bowl and add the back fat, sea salt, thyme and bay and season generously with pepper. Mix well.

4 Spoon the sausagemeat into a large piping bag fitted with a large plain plastic nozzle and squeeze gently to remove any excess air. Wrinkle the open end of a sausage casing on to and up the nozzle and, holding the skin on to the nozzle, squeeze the filling into the casing to create a long sausage. (You may need to do this in 2 or 3 stages.) Twist or knot the long sausage at intervals to make 8 large or 12 small sausages. Alternatively, make small patties to cook directly on the barbecue.
5 To make the mustard aïoli, place the garlic and egg yolks in a food processor or blender, add the lemon juice and

process briefly to mix. With the motor running, gradually add the olive oil in a thin stream until the mixture forms a thick cream. Scrape the aïoli into a bowl, season with salt and pepper and stir in the mustard, adding more lemon juice if needed. Set aside.
6 Place the sausages on the barbecue grill over moderately low heat and cook, turning frequently, for 10–15 minutes until cooked through. Serve hot with the aïoli.

Serves 4
Preparation time: 1 hour
Cooking time: 10–15 minutes

Poultry and Game

Chicken and Pancetta Kebabs with Parsley Pesto

4 boneless chicken thighs, total weight 500 g/1lb, each cut into 4	PARSLEY PESTO:
1 tablespoon chopped fresh rosemary	50 g/2 oz fresh flat leaf parsley
50 ml/2 fl oz olive oil	25 g/1 oz pine nuts
50 ml/2 fl oz freshly squeezed lemon juice	2 garlic cloves, crushed
2 garlic cloves, crushed	125 ml/4 fl oz olive oil
12 very thin slices of pancetta or streaky bacon	25 g/1 oz Parmesan cheese, grated
	salt and pepper

1 Mix together the rosemary, olive oil, lemon juice and crushed garlic in a bowl, add the chicken pieces, cover and leave to marinate for 2–4 hours.

2 To make the parsley pesto, place the parsley, pine nuts and garlic in a food processor or blender and work until finely chopped. With the motor running, gradually add the olive oil in a thin stream until amalgamated. Scrape the pesto into a bowl and stir in the Parmesan, season to taste with salt and black pepper.

3 Remove the chicken from the marinade and wrap a slice of pancetta around each piece. Thread 2 pieces of chicken on to each skewer and place on the barbecue grill. Cook for 10–15 minutes, turning and basting until cooked. Serve with the parsley pesto and a rocket and yellow cherry tomato salad.

Serves 4
Preparation time: 20 minutes, plus marinating
Cooking time: 10–15 minutes

Chicken Tikka Kebabs and Naan Bread

- 4 naan breads (see right)
- 750 g/1½ lb skinless, boneless chicken breasts, cut into 2.5 cm/1 inch cubes
- lemon or lime wedges, to garnish

MARINADE:

- 1 onion, roughly chopped
- 2.5 cm/1 inch piece of fresh root ginger, peeled and roughly chopped
- 2 garlic cloves, crushed
- 150 ml/¼ pint natural yogurt
- 1–2 red chillies, deseeded and chopped
- 2 teaspoons ground coriander
- 1 teaspoon ground cumin
- ½ teaspoon turmeric
- juice of 1 lemon
- 1 teaspoon salt

1 Make the naan bread (see right). Leave to cool, then wrap in foil.
2 To make the marinade, place the onion, ginger, garlic, yogurt, chillies, coriander, cumin, turmeric, lemon juice and salt in a food processor or blender and purée until smooth.
3 Place the chicken cubes in a shallow bowl, pour over the marinade and toss well to coat. Cover and marinate in the refrigerator overnight.
4 Remove the chicken with a slotted spoon and pour the marinade into a jug.
5 Cook the kebabs on an oiled barbecue over hot coals for 6 minutes on each side, basting with the marinade.
6 While the kebabs are cooking, place the parcels of naan bread on the edge

of the barbecue grill to heat through.
7 Serve the kebabs with the naan and garnish with wedges of lemon or lime.

Serves 4
Preparation time: 30 minutes, plus marinating
Cooking time: 12–15 minutes

Naan Bread

- 1 teaspon dried yeast
- 1 teaspoon sugar
- 50 ml/2 fl oz warm milk
- 250 g/8 oz plain flour
- ½ teaspoon salt
- 1 tablespoon vegetable oil
- 1 egg, beaten
- 4 tablespoons natural yogurt

1 Sprinkle the yeast and sugar over the milk. Mix, cover and keep warm for 15–20 minutes, until frothy.
2 Sift the flour and salt into a large bowl, make a well in the centre and add the oil, egg, yogurt and yeast mixture. Mix, gradually incorporating the flour until the dough forms a soft ball. Turn out on to a floured surface, knead for 10 minutes until smooth, then place in an oiled bowl. Cover and leave to rise in a warm place for 1 hour or until the dough has doubled in bulk.
3 Knock down the dough, then knead for 5 minutes. Divide into 4 pieces, then roll each one into a 20 x 12 cm/ 8 x 5 inch tear shape, place on an oiled baking sheet, cover and leave to rise for 25 minutes in a warm place.
4 Heat a cast-iron pan, cook each piece of dough for 3 minutes, turn and place them under a grill for 2–3 minutes, until golden and spotty.

Serves 4
Preparation time: 2 hours 10 minutes
Cooking time: 12–15 minutes

Chicken and Herb Crépinettes

These tasty smooth chicken burgers are wrapped in lacy caul fat. This not only bastes the meat and protects it from drying out but also gives the burgers added flavour. Caul fat is available from good butchers.

- 125 g/4 oz piece of day-old bread, crusts removed
- 300 ml/½ pint milk
- 500 g/1 lb skinless, boneless chicken, cubed
- 1 egg white
- 150 ml/¼ pint double cream
- 2 shallots, finely chopped
- 2 teaspoons chopped fresh parsley
- 2 teaspoons chopped fresh thyme
- 300 g/10 oz caul fat
- 8–12 sage leaves
- salt and pepper

PEACH RELISH:
- ripe peaches
- 2 tablespoons chopped red onion
- 1–2 green chillies, deseeded and chopped
- ½ tablespoon walnut oil
- salt and pepper

1 Place the bread in a bowl, pour over the milk and leave to stand for about 10 minutes. Squeeze the bread, discarding the milk, and place in a food processor. Add the chicken and process to a smooth paste.

2 Spoon the mixture into a bowl and stir in the egg white, cream, shallots and chopped parsley and thyme. Season with salt and pepper.

3 Divide the mixture into 8 and shape into burgers. Soak the caul fat in warm water for 5 minutes, drain and stretch it out on a chopping board. Cut out 8 x 15 cm/6 inch squares. Place 1–2 sage leaves in the centre of each square and top with a chicken burger. Fold the caul fat over and secure the back of the crépinettes with a cocktail stick. Transfer the crépinettes to a baking sheet, cover and leave to set in the refrigerator.

4 Meanwhile, to make the peach relish, score a cross on the top of each peach. Plunge them into a saucepan of boiling water for 20 seconds, then transfer them to a bowl of cold water with a slotted spoon. Slip off the skins, cut the peaches in half and discard the stones. Chop the flesh finely and place it in a bowl with the onion, chillies and walnut oil. Mix well and season to taste with salt and pepper.

5 Remove the crépinettes from the refrigerator 20–30 minutes before cooking, then place on an oiled barbecue grill. Cook for 15–20 minutes, turning frequently. Serve at once, with the peach relish.

Serves 4
Preparation time: 50 minutes
Cooking time: 15–20 minutes

Goat's Cheese Stuffed Chicken with a Tomato and Chive Vinaigrette

- 4 x 175–250 g/6–8 oz boneless chicken breasts
- 125 g/4 oz soft goats' cheese
- 25 g/1 oz walnuts, finely chopped
- 2 tablespoons chopped flat leaf parsley
- 2 tablespoons Dijon mustard
- 3 tablespoons olive oil
- 1 garlic clove, crushed
- salt and pepper
- young leaf spinach, to serve

TOMATO AND CHIVE VINAIGRETTE:
- 15 g/½ oz chives, chopped
- 100 ml/3½ fl oz extra virgin olive oil
- juice and finely grated rind of 1 lime
- 500 g/1 lb ripe tomatoes, skinned, deseeded and chopped

1 Pull away the small fillets from the flesh of the chicken breasts. Place each fillet in between 2 pieces of clingfilm and flatten gently with a rolling pin. Set aside. Place each chicken breast skin side down, insert a small knife into the thickest part of the flesh and slice along to create a pocket, being careful not to make any holes.
2 To make the stuffing, place the goats' cheese, walnuts and parsley in a small bowl and mix well. Season to taste with salt and pepper. Divide the mixture into 4 and spoon a quarter of the mixture into each chicken breast pocket. Place the small chicken fillet over the top and draw the edges of the chicken breast around it. Place the chicken breasts on a tray, cover and leave to rest in the refrigerator for 30 minutes.
3 To make the tomato and chive vinaigrette, place the chives in a food processor or blender with the oil and work until smooth. Pour into a small bowl and stir in the lime juice and rind. Season with salt and pepper and gently stir in the chopped tomatoes.
4 Mix together the mustard, olive oil and garlic in a small bowl. Brush the chicken breasts all over with the mustard glaze, then place them, skin side down, on a well oiled barbecue grill and cook for 15–20 minutes, turning once and basting occasionally with the remaining glaze. Serve the chicken breasts on a bed of fresh young leaf spinach with the vinaigrette sprinkled around.

Serves 4
Preparation time: 20 minutes, plus resting
Cooking time: 15–20 minutes

Honey and Orange Chicken Sticks with Toasted Corn Salsa

- 4 x 175 g/6 oz boneless chicken breasts

TOASTED CORN SALSA:

- 2 corn cobs, husks and inner silks removed
- 3 tablespoons sunflower oil
- 4 spring onions, chopped
- 3 tablespoons chopped fresh coriander
- 2 teaspoons toasted sesame seeds
- 1 tablespoon freshly squeezed lime juice
- 1 tablespoon light soy sauce
- 1 teaspoon sesame oil
- salt and pepper

MARINADE:

- 2.5 cm/1 inch piece of fresh root ginger, peeled and very finely grated
- 2 garlic cloves, crushed
- finely grated rind and juice of 1 orange
- 2 tablespoons olive oil
- 2 tablespoons honey

1 First make the marinade. Place the ginger, garlic, orange rind and juice and honey in a large bowl and mix together. Cut each chicken breast into 8 long thin strips and coat thoroughly with the marinade. Cover and leave to marinate for 1–2 hours. If using wooden skewers soak them in cold water for 30 minutes.

2 To make the toasted corn salsa, brush the corn cobs with 2 tablespoons of the oil and place under a preheated grill. Cook for 10–15 minutes, turning frequently, until the cobs are charred and the kernels are tender. Remove from the heat and when cool enough to handle remove the kernels from the cobs with a sharp knife. (Alternatively, cook the cobs on the barbecue, then remove the kernels.)

3 Place the kernels in a bowl, add the remaining oil, spring onions, coriander, sesame seeds, lime juice and soy sauce and season to taste. Set aside.

4 Remove the chicken strips from the marinade and thread 2 pieces on to each skewer. Place the skewers on the barbecue grill and cook for 2–3 minutes on each side until cooked through, basting with any remaining marinade. Serve with the toasted corn salsa and a green salad.

Serves 4
Preparation time: 20 minutes, plus marinating
Cooking time: 12–16 minutes

South-east Asian Grilled Chicken with Pineapple and Peanut Relish

Like many of the best barbecue recipes, this one comes from South-east Asia.

- 4 part-boned chicken breasts
- lime wedges, to garnish

MARINADE:

- 2 sticks of lemon grass, finely chopped
- juice of 2 limes
- 2 red chillies, deseeded and chopped
- 3 garlic cloves, crushed
- 2.5 cm/1 inch piece of fresh root ginger, finely chopped
- 2 tablespoons soft dark brown sugar
- 2 tablespoons chopped fresh coriander
- 150 ml/¼ pint coconut milk

PINEAPPLE AND PEANUT RELISH:

- 1 small pineapple, peeled, cored and finely chopped
- 1 red onion, chopped
- 3 tablespoons freshly squeezed lime juice
- 1 garlic clove, crushed
- 1 tablespoon light soy sauce
- 25 g/1 oz roasted unsalted peanuts, chopped

1 Cut 3 diagonal slits in each chicken breast. Place the chicken in a shallow dish large enough to hold all the breasts in a single layer.

2 To make the marinade, place all the ingredients in a food processor or blender and purée until smooth. Pour over the chicken, cover and leave to marinate for 1–1½ hours.

3 Meanwhile, to make the pineapple and peanut relish, mix all the ingredients in a bowl, cover and set aside.

4 Remove the chicken breasts from the marinade, reserving the marinade. Cook the chicken on an oiled barbecue over hot coals for 25–30 minutes or until tender and cooked through.

5 Transfer the chicken to individual plates, garnish with lime wedges and serve with the pineapple and peanut relish. Steamed mixed rice is also a good accompaniment.

Serves 4
Preparation time: 30 minutes, plus marinating
Cooking time: 25–30 minutes

Spatchcocked Poussins

Spatchcocking is a term used for splitting and flattening a bird for cooking. The method is ideal for barbecuing as it speeds up the cooking process and cooks the meat evenly. Here a sun-dried tomato and basil butter is inserted under the skin to baste the flesh while the chicken cooks and to keep it moist and succulent.

- 3 sun-dried tomatoes in oil, drained and chopped, with oil reserved
- 125 g/4 oz butter, softened
- 3 tablespoons roughly chopped fresh basil
- 4 poussins, about 500 g/1 lb each
- salt and pepper

1 Place the sun-dried tomatoes in a food processor or blender, add the butter and basil and purée until smooth. Transfer to a bowl. Alternatively, chop the tomatoes and basil finely and beat with the butter in a bowl. Cover and chill.
2 Place each poussin breast side down on a board and, with poultry shears or strong kitchen scissors, cut down on either side of the backbone and remove it. Turn the poussin over and open it out, then flatten it by pressing down hard on the breastbone with the heel of your hand.
3 Lift the skin covering the breast and gently push your fingers between the flesh and skin to make a pocket. Divide the sun-dried tomato and basil

butter equally among the poussins, pushing it underneath the skin.
4 Working with one bird at a time, thread a skewer through a drumstick, under the breastbone and through the second drumstick. Thread another skewer through the wings catching the flap of skin underneath. (This helps to flatten the bird for even cooking.)
5 Brush the poussins with the reserved oil from the tomatoes, place on a oiled barbecue grill and cook for 15–20 minutes until the juices run clear. Suitable accompaniments would be a chicory and frisé salad, and a vegetable such as grilled, sliced fennel.

Serves 4
Preparation time: 25 minutes
Cooking time: approximately 15–20 minutes

VARIATION

Tarragon and Lemon Butter

Use in place of the sun-dried tomato and basil butter. The quantity is sufficient for 4 poussins or 1 chicken.

- 125 g/4 oz butter, softened
- 3 tablespoons chopped fresh tarragon
- 2 shallots, very finely chopped
- finely grated rind and juice of 1 lemon
- salt and pepper

1 Place all the ingredients in a food processor or a mixing bowl and beat together, then continue as for the sun-dried tomato and basil butter in the main recipe.

Guinea Fowl with Mushroom Stuffing

- 1 x 1–1.5 kg/2–3 lb guinea fowl
- butter or oil, for brushing

MUSHROOM STUFFING:

- 25 g/1 oz dried porcini mushrooms, soaked for 30 minutes in warm water to cover
- 50 g/2 oz butter
- 2 shallots, finely chopped
- 1 garlic clove, crushed
- 250 g/8 oz field mushrooms, finely chopped
- 2 tablespoons chopped fresh parsley
- salt and pepper

1 To make the stuffing, drain the mushrooms through a sieve lined with kitchen paper. Reserve the liquid. Rinse the mushrooms under cold water, drain again, then chop finely.
2 Melt the butter in a saucepan. Add the shallots and garlic and cook gently for 2–3 minutes until softened but not coloured. Add both types of mushrooms and cook for 4–5 minutes more. Stir in the reserved mushroom liquid and boil hard until all the liquid has evaporated. Off the heat, stir in the parsley and add salt and pepper to taste. Cool slightly.
3 To open out the guinea fowl, snip down either side of the backbone and remove it. Place the bird on a clean surface, breast up. Press down firmly with the heel of your hand to break the breastbone and flatten the bird.
4 Lift and loosen the skin gently, easing it away from the breast and leg meat with your fingers. Take care not to make any holes. Spoon the stuffing under the skin and spread it out evenly. Pull the skin back tightly over the bird and secure underneath with a skewer or cocktail sticks.
5 Brush the guinea fowl with a little butter or oil. Cook breast side down on an oiled barbecue grill over hot coals for 10–15 minutes. Turn the bird over and cook for 10–15 minutes more. Continue cooking, turning the bird occasionally until the juices run clear when the thickest part of a thigh is pierced with a fork. Transfer to a platter, cover with tented foil and keep hot while preparing the apple rings.
6 Carve the guinea fowl and serve with the apples rings.

Serves 4
Preparation time: 35 minutes, plus soaking
Cooking time: 40–50 minutes

Cidered Apple Rings

- 25 g/1 oz butter
- 3 red dessert apples, cored and sliced into 5 mm/¼ inch rings
- 250 ml/8 fl oz dry cider
- 2 tablespoons Calvados (optional)
- 250 ml/8 fl oz crème fraîche
- salt and pepper

1 Heat the butter in a large frying pan, add the apples and cook for 4–5 minutes until golden. Remove the apple rings with a slotted spoon. Add the cider, raise the heat and cook until reduced by half. Stir in the Calvados and crème fraîche and cook for 3–4 minutes until thickened. Return the apples to the pan and heat through.

Serves 4
Preparation time: 5 minutes
Cooking time: 10 minutes

Maple Duck with Apricot Pecan Chutney

- 4 x 200–250 g/7–8 oz duck breasts
- 4 tablespoons maple syrup
- 1 teaspoon vanilla essence
- juice and finely grated rind of 1 orange
- juice and finely grated rind of 1 lime

APRICOT PECAN CHUTNEY:

- 250 g/8 oz dried apricots
- 1 large onion, sliced

- 50 g/2 oz raisins
- 50 g/2 oz brown sugar
- 300 ml/½ pint cider vinegar
- 1 teaspoon yellow mustard seeds
- ¼ teaspoon ground ginger
- ¼ teaspoon cayenne
- 1 tablespoon salt
- 50 g/2 oz shelled pecan nuts, chopped

1 To make the apricot pecan chutney, place all the ingredients, except the pecans, in a heavy-based saucepan or preserving pan. Bring to a boil, then reduce the heat to very low and simmer very gently for 45 minutes or until thick. Stir frequently to prevent sticking. Stir in the pecans and pour into sterilised jars whilst still hot. Cover and seal.
2 If using wooden skewers, soak 12 skewers in cold water for 30 minutes. Using a sharp knife, cut away any excess fat and score the skin of the duck in a criss-cross pattern. Cut the breasts into 3.5 cm/1½ inch cubes and thread on to the skewers. In a small bowl, mix together the maple syrup, vanilla, fruit juice and rind.
3 Place the skewers on a preheated barbecue and seal quickly for 2 minutes on each side. Remove from the heat and brush with the glaze. Return the duck to the barbecue and continue cooking , turning and basting frequently with any remaining marinade, for 5–8 minutes until cooked through. Serve immediately on a bed of curly endive.

Serves 4
Preparation time: 30 minutes
Cooking time: 7–10 minutes, plus 45 minutes for the chutney

Venison Cutlets with Red Juniper Pears

Pears in red wine, usually a dessert, are also excellent with rich venison.

- 4 firm dessert pears
- 2 tablespoons lemon juice
- 300 ml/½ pint red wine
- 6 juniper berries, crushed
- pared rind of 1 lemon, cut into julienne strips
- 1 stick of cinnamon
- oil or melted butter, for brushing
- 3 tablespoons redcurrant jelly
- 8 venison cutlets

1 Peel the pears, then halve them lengthways and remove each core with a melon baller. Brush the flesh with the lemon juice to prevent the pears from discolouring.

2 Combine the wine, juniper berries, lemon rind and cinnamon stick in a saucepan. Bring to the boil, add the pears, cover and simmer gently for 10 minutes or until tender.

3 Transfer the pears to a bowl with a slotted spoon and set aside. Stir the redcurrant jelly into the liquid remaining in the pan and boil until reduced by half. Pour over the pears and leave to cool.

4 Brush the venison with a little oil or butter. Cook on an oiled barbecue grill over hot coals for 2–3 minutes on each side. To serve, place 2 cutlets on each plate and add a portion of pears. Serve with sprigs of watercress.

Serves 4
Preparation time: 20 minutes
Cooking time: 6–8 minutes

Vegetable Dishes

Black Bean Kebabs with Mango Relish

125 g/4 oz dried black beans

3 tablespoons olive oil

1 onion, very finely chopped

1 garlic clove, crushed

1 red chilli, deseeded and finely chopped

1 teaspoon ground coriander

1 tablespoon chopped fresh coriander

2 medium courgettes

24 mixed red and yellow cherry tomatoes

MANGO RELISH:

1 ripe mango, peeled and stoned

1 small onion, grated

1 red chilli, deseeded and finely chopped

1 cm/½ inch piece of fresh root ginger, peeled and grated

salt and pepper

1 Place the beans in a bowl with cold water to cover. Soak overnight, then tip into a colander and rinse well under cold running water. Transfer to a saucepan and cover with fresh water. Bring to the boil. Boil vigorously for 10 minutes, then lower the heat and simmer for about 40–50 minutes until tender. Drain well and set the beans aside.

2 To make the mango relish, place the flesh in a bowl and mash lightly. Add the onion, chilli and ginger and mix well. Season with a little salt and pepper and set aside.

3 Heat 2 tablespoons of the oil in a pan. Add the onion, garlic and chilli and cook for 5–10 minutes until the onion is softened. Add the ground coriander and cook for 1–2 minutes more. Turn the onion and spice mixture into a bowl, add the drained beans and fresh coriander and mash well. Form the mixture into 24 balls.

4 Cut the courgettes lengthways into strips and brush with the remaining oil. Thread the bean balls on metal skewers alternating with the cherry tomatoes and weaving the courgette strips in between. Cook the kebabs on a well-oiled barbecue grill over moderately hot coals for 4 minutes on each side. Serve with the mango relish and rice.

Serves 4

Preparation time: 1 hour 20 minutes, plus overnight soaking

Cooking time: 8 minutes

Rabbit with Oyster Mushrooms and Hazelnut Butter

- 1 rabbit, cut into 8 portions
- 125 g/4 oz butter, slightly softened
- 50 g/2 oz hazelnuts, toasted and chopped
- salt and pepper

SKEWERED MUSHROOMS:

- 250 g/8 oz oyster mushrooms, trimmed
- 8 slices of pancetta
- 25 g/1 oz butter, melted

MARINADE:

- 300 ml/½ pint dry white wine
- 2 tablespoons chopped fresh tarragon
- 3 tablespoons olive or hazelnut oil
- strips of rind from 1 lemon
- 1 teaspoon black peppercorns

1 Place the rabbit portions in a single layer in a shallow dish. To make the marinade, mix the wine, tarragon, olive or hazelnut oil, lemon rind and peppercorns in a jug, pour over the rabbit and toss to coat. Cover the dish and marinate for 6–8 hours or overnight in the refrigerator.

2 Beat the butter until light and fluffy, stir in the hazelnuts, then season to taste. Place a 25 x 25 cm/10 x 10 inch square piece of greaseproof paper on a work surface. Spoon the butter evenly down the centre, roll over the paper to form a long thin sausage, then twist the ends and place in the refrigerator to harden.

3 Shortly before cooking the rabbit, prepare the skewered mushrooms. If using wooden skewers, soak them in cold water for 30 minutes. Thread the mushrooms on to 8 skewers, winding the pancetta between them. Brush with the melted butter.

4 Drain the rabbit and reserve the marinade. Cook on an oiled grill over hot coals for 20–25 minutes or until tender. Baste frequently with the marinade. Add the mushroom skewers to the grill for the final 5 minutes, turning frequently.

5 Place 2 rabbit portions on each plate, add a mushroom skewer and dot with slices of the hazelnut butter. Serve with grilled celery, if liked.

Serves 4
Preparation time: 10 minutes, plus marinating
Cooking time: 20–25 minutes

Fennel, Lemon and Black Olive Kebabs

- **2 fennel bulbs**
- **1 lemon**

LEMON AND OLIVE DRESSING:

- **2 tablespoons fresh lemon juice**
- **1 garlic clove, crushed**
- **8 tablespoons extra virgin olive oil**
- **75 g/3 oz pitted black olives, finely chopped**
- **sea salt and pepper**

1 First make the lemon and olive dressing. Whisk together the lemon juice, garlic and 6 tablespoons of the olive oil in a bowl. Stir in the chopped black olives and season with sea salt and pepper.

2 Cut the fennel bulbs lengthways into 8 wedges, making sure each wedge is attached to a little of the core. Cut the lemon into 8 wedges.

3 Thread the fennel and lemon wedges alternately on to 4 skewers and brush all over with the remaining olive oil.

Place the kebabs on an oiled barbecue grill and cook for about 4 minutes on each side. Remove from the heat and serve drizzled with the lemon and olive dressing.

Serves 4
Preparation time: 15 minutes
Cooking time: 8 minutes

Red Chilli Polenta Chips and Grilled Garlic Skewers

Polenta is the Italian name for the bright yellow cornmeal known in the United States as cornmeal mush.

- **750 ml/1¼ pints water**
- **1 teaspoon salt**
- **250 g/8 oz polenta**
- **50 g/2 oz finely grated Parmesan cheese**
- **8 sun-dried tomato halves in oil, drained and finely chopped**
- **4 large red chillies, grilled, peeled, deseeded and finely chopped (see page 62)**
- **12 garlic cloves, unpeeled**
- **6 tablespoons olive oil**

1 Bring the measured water and salt to the boil in a large pan. Reduce the heat slightly and add the polenta in a thin stream, beating all the time. Cook, stirring constantly, for 20–30 minutes, until the mixture comes away from the sides of the pan.

2 Immediately stir in the Parmesan, sun-dried tomatoes and chopped red chillies. Tip the polenta out on to a board or baking sheet. Leave to cool, then cut into chunky chips.

3 Bring a small pan of water to the boil and add the garlic cloves. Reduce the heat and simmer for 10 minutes. Drain. When cool enough to handle, skewer 3 garlic cloves on to each of 4 presoaked wooden cocktail sticks.

4 Brush the polenta chips and garlic skewers with the oil and cook on the barbecue grill for about 3 minutes on each side until the garlic is soft and the polenta is charred and golden.

Serves 4
Preparation time: 10 minutes
Cooking time: 25–35 minutes

Polenta and Vegetable Terrine with Roasted Tomatoes

- 4 tablespoons olive oil, plus extra for brushing
- 1 red pepper
- 250 g/8 oz mushrooms, quartered
- 2 red onions, cut into small wedges
- 125 g/4 oz baby courgettes, cut in half lengthways
- 125 g/4 oz baby carrots
- 125 g/4 oz French beans, topped and tailed
- 125 g/4 oz broccoli, cut into florets

- 1.5 litres/2½ pints water
- 300 g/10 oz polenta
- 50 g/2 oz Parmesan cheese, grated, plus extra for sprinkling
- 2 garlic cloves, crushed
- 8 ripe plum tomatoes, cut in half lengthways
- 50 g/2 oz black olives
- salt and pepper

1 Brush a 1.25 kg/2½ lb loaf tin with olive oil. Place the red pepper under a preheated grill for 10 minutes until blistered and charred. Place in a polythene bag, close lightly and set aside to cool. Peel off the charred skin; cut the pepper in half and remove the seeds. Cut the flesh into 2.5 cm/1 inch strips.
2 Heat half of the oil in a frying pan, add the mushrooms and onions, cover and cook for 2–3 minutes. Remove with a slotted spoon and drain on kitchen paper.
3 Blanch the remaining vegetables in separate saucepans of boiling salted water until crisp and tender. Drain, refresh under cold running water and drain again.
4 Bring the measured water to the boil in a large saucepan. Add a pinch of salt, then pour in the polenta in a thin steady stream, stirring all the time. Continue to stir the mixture, beating it as it thickens, for about 20 minutes until the mixture leaves the sides of the pan. Remove from the heat, add all the vegetables and the grated Parmesan, mix well and spoon into the loaf tin. Level the surface and set aside. When the polenta loaf is completely cold, turn it out of the tin and cut into 2 cm/¾ inch slices. Brush each side with a little of the remaining oil.
5 Mix the garlic with the remaining oil, brush over the tomatoes and season to taste.
6 Place the terrine slices on an oiled barbecue grill over moderately hot coals. Add the tomatoes, cut side down. Cook the terrine and tomatoes for 6–8 minutes, turning once. (Be sure the terrine slices have a crispy surface before turning them over.)
7 Serve the terrine on individual plates topped with the tomato halves. Garnish with the olives and serve with more grated Parmesan.

Serves 6–8
Preparation time: 1 hour 10 minutes
Cooking time: 6–8 minutes

VARIATION

Polenta and Vegetable Kebabs

1 Make the polenta as in the main recipe. As soon as it leaves the sides of the pan, pour out into a mound on a board. Leave to cool, then cut into 2.5 cm/1 inch cubes.
2 Thread the cubes of polenta on to skewers, alternating with red onions, mushrooms, squares of red pepper, thickly sliced courgettes and blanched carrots. Brush with olive oil. Grill for about 5–6 minutes on each side over moderately hot coals until the vegetables are tender and the polenta cubes are golden.
3 Serve with the grilled tomato halves and sprinkle with Parmesan.

Charred Grilled Peppers and Goats' Cheese with Grilled Chilli Relish

- 2 red peppers
- 2 yellow peppers
- 2 individual goats' cheeses

- 1 tablespoon fresh thyme leaves
- 2 tablespoons extra virgin olive oil
- 25 g/1 oz pitted black olives, finely chopped
- cracked black pepper

CHILLI RELISH:

- 6 large red chillies
- 2 tablespoons lime juice
- 2 garlic cloves, crushed
- 3 tablespoons chopped fresh flat leaf parsley or coriander
- sea salt

1 First make the chilli relish. Put the chillies on to a baking sheet and place under a preheated grill. Leave to cook for about 5–10 minutes, turning occasionally until well charred and blistered all over. Place the chillies in a plastic bag and tie the top, leave to cool. When cool enough to handle, remove the stalks, cut the chillies in half and remove the seeds. Roughly chop the flesh.

2 Place the chillies in a mortar and pound with a pestle. (Alternatively crush in a spice grinder) Stir in the remaining ingredients and season with salt. Set aside.

3 Cut the peppers in half lengthways and remove the seeds. Leave the stalks attached but trim away any white membrane. Place the peppers on a barbecue grill cut side down and cook for 8–10 minutes until well charred. Cut each goat's cheese into 4 slices. Turn the peppers over, place a slice of goats' cheese in the centre, sprinkle with the thyme and olive oil and leave to cook for a further 10 minutes or until the peppers have softened and the goats' cheese has melted.

4 Serve sprinkled with the chopped black olives and cracked black pepper and serve with the chilli relish.

Serves 4
Preparation time: 20 minutes
Cooking time: 12–25 minutes

Grilled Haloumi Wrapped in Radicchio

- 250 g/8 oz haloumi cheese
- 1½ tablespoons chopped fresh oregano
- 2 tablespoons extra virgin olive oil
- 1 garlic clove, crushed
- juice of ½ lemon
- 1 large radicchio lettuce
- salt and pepper

1 Cut the haloumi into 4 equal pieces or small cubes. Mix together the oregano, olive oil, garlic and lemon juice in a bowl, add the haloumi pieces and toss to coat.

2 Remove any stalk and the core from the radicchio and gently pull the leaves apart. Lay 3–4 leaves on a work surface and place a quarter of the haloumi mixture in the centre. Wrap the radicchio around and then over-wrap in a piece of heavy duty foil. Repeat with the remaining radicchio and cheese mixture.

3 Place the parcels on a barbecue grill over moderately low heat and cook for 3–4 minutes on each side. Remove from the heat and serve immediately with new potatoes.

Serves 4
Preparation time: 10 minutes
Cooking time: 6–8 minutes

Grilled Radicchio with Pears and Roquefort

The slight bitterness of the radicchio combines well with citrus-sweet baked pears and creamy sharp cheese to make a dish which is equally suitable as an unusual starter or as a ending to a rich meal. Sadly the ruby red colour of the radicchio is somewhat lost in cooking but the flavour is delicious none the less.

- 4 ripe pears, such as Conference
- finely grated rind and juice of 2 oranges
- 4 tablespoons clear honey
- 4 small radicchio

- 1 tablespoon walnut oil
- 125 g/4 oz Roquefort cheese, crumbled
- pepper

1 Cut each pear lengthways into quarters and remove the core. Arrange the pears in a single layer on a large sheet of double foil, turning up the edges slightly.
2 Mix the orange rind and juice and honey in a jug. Pour over the pears.
3 Bring up the edges of the foil and press together to seal. Place the parcel on a barbecue grill over moderately hot coals and cook for about 15–20 minutes or until the pears are tender.
4 About 6 minutes before the pears are ready, cook the radicchio. Cut each radicchio into quarters, brush with the walnut oil and cook on an oiled barbecue grill for 2–3 minutes on each side.
5 To serve, divide the pears and cooking juices among 4 plates. Add 4 radicchio quarters to each portion. Sprinkle the radicchio with the crumbled Roquefort and a little pepper.

Serves 4
Preparation time: 5 minutes
Cooking time: 15–20 minutes

VARIATION

Pears and Roquefort with Almonds

Prepare the pears as for the main recipe. Before closing the foil parcel, sprinkle 125 g/4 oz crumbled Roquefort cheese over the pears. To serve, scatter toasted almonds over each portion.

Hot Asparagus with Balsamic Vinegar and Tomato Dressing

Tender young asparagus is perfect for the barbecue as it cooks quickly and easily. Serve this dish as a starter, with lots of warm bread to mop up the juices, while you prepare the main course.

- 500 g/1 lb young asparagus spears, trimmed
- 50 g/2 oz pine nuts, toasted
- 25 g/1 oz Parmesan cheese, shaved into thin slivers
- sea salt flakes and pepper

BALSAMIC VINEGAR AND TOMATO DRESSING:

- 2 tablespoons balsamic vinegar
- 1–2 garlic cloves, crushed
- 375 g/12 oz tomatoes, skinned, deseeded and chopped
- 7 tablespoons olive oil

1 To make the dressing, mix the vinegar, garlic, tomatoes and 5 tablespoons of the olive oil in a bowl. Set aside.

2 Brush the asparagus with the remaining oil and cook on an oiled barbecue grill over moderately hot coals for 5–6 minutes until tender.

3 Divide the grilled asparagus among 4 warmed serving plates. Spoon over the balsamic vinegar and tomato dressing, top with the pine nuts and Parmesan slivers and sprinkle with the sea salt and pepper. Serve at once.

Serves 4
Preparation time: 15 minutes
Cooking time: 5–6 minutes

Baby Aubergines with Herbed Greek Yogurt

Mini vegetables are perfect for cooking whole on the barbecue as they are usually both sweet and tender and so cook speedily. Little aubergines are usually available from most major ethnic markets. Make the yogurt mixture well ahead, so the flavours blend thoroughly, then serve these baby aubergines with warm pitta bread lightly toasted on the grill.

- 12 baby aubergines
- 3 tablespoons olive oil
- salt and pepper

HERBED GREEK YOGURT:

- 2 tablespoons chopped fresh parsley
- 2 tablespoons chopped fresh dill
- 2 tablespoons chopped fresh mint
- 1 small red onion, finely chopped
- 2 garlic cloves, crushed
- 75 g/3 oz Kalamata olives, pitted and sliced
- 2 teaspoons fennel seeds, crushed
- 1 tablespoon capers, chopped
- 15 g/½ oz gherkins, finely chopped
- finely grated rind and juice of 1 lime
- 150 ml/¼ pint strained Greek yogurt
- salt and pepper

1 To make the herbed Greek yogurt, mix all the ingredients and set aside.
2 Slice all the baby aubergines in half lengthways, leaving the stalks attached.
3 Using a small brush, coat the aubergines with the olive oil. Cook on an oiled barbecue grill over moderately hot coals for about 2–3 minutes on each side.
4 To serve, place the aubergines on a serving dish or plate and spoon over the herbed yogurt.

Serves 4
Preparation time: 20 minutes
Cooking time: 6 minutes

Whole Baked Sweetcorn with Skorthalia

Cobs of tender young corn, preferably freshly picked ones, are delicious when spread with this rich Greek garlic sauce.

- 4 whole corn cobs, with husks

SKORTHALIA:

- 50 g/2 oz fresh white breadcrumbs
- 75 g/3 oz ground almonds
- 4 garlic cloves, crushed
- 2 tablespoons lemon juice
- 150 ml/¼ pint extra virgin olive oil
- salt and pepper

1 To make the skorthalia, place the breadcrumbs in a bowl and cover with water. Soak for 5 minutes, then squeeze out the excess liquid and place the crumbs in a food processor or blender. Add the ground almonds, garlic and 1 tablespoon of the lemon juice. Process until mixed. With the motor running, gradually add the olive oil in a thin steady stream until the mixture resembles mayonnaise. Add more lemon juice and season to taste with salt and pepper.

2 Pull down the outer leaves of the sweetcorn husks and remove the inner silks. Pull the leaves back over the corn kernels. Place on a barbecue grill over hot coals. Cook for about 30–40 minutes until the kernels are juicy and easily come away from the core.

3 To serve, pull back the leaves of the corn cobs and spread with the skorthalia.

Serves 4
Preparation time: 15 minutes
Cooking time: 30–40 minutes

VARIATION

Grilled Baby Corn Cobs

If you are unable to obtain whole corn cobs, use baby sweetcorn instead.

Thread 500 g/1 lb baby corn cobs on to skewers, brush them with a little olive oil and cook on an oiled barbecue grill over hot coals, turning frequently, for 4–6 minutes. Serve with the skorthalia.

Barbecued Potato Wedges with Sun-Dried Tomato Aïoli

- 4 large potatoes
- 4 tablespoons olive oil
- paprika
- sea salt flakes

SUN-DRIED TOMATO AIOLI:

- 4–6 garlic cloves, crushed
- 2 egg yolks
- juice ½ lemon, plus extra to taste
- 300 ml/½ pint extra virgin olive oil
- 8 sun–dried tomato halves in oil, drained and finely chopped

1 If using wooden skewers, soak them in cold water for 30 minutes.

2 Place the whole, unpeeled potatoes in a large pan of cold water, bring to the boil, reduce the heat and simmer for 15–20 minutes or until just tender. Drain, and when cool enough to handle, cut each potato into large wedges.

3 To make the sun-dried tomato aïoli, place the garlic and egg yolks in a food processor or blender, add the lemon juice and process briefly to mix. With the motor running, gradually add the oil in a thin stream until the mixture forms a thick cream. Scrape into a bowl and stir in the sun-dried tomatoes, season with salt and pepper, adding more lemon juice if liked.

4 Brush the potato wedges with the oil, sprinkle with a little paprika and skewer or lay the potato wedges on a barbecue grill and cook for 5–6 minutes, turning frequently until golden brown all over. Serve with the aïoli.

Serves 4

Preparation time: 15–20 minutes
Cooking time: 20–25 minutes

Salad
Dishes

Carrot and Celeriac Salad

Crisp carrots and nutty celeriac blend well with a mild peppery mustard dressing.

250 g/8 oz carrots
250 g/8 oz celeriac
6 spring onions, finely sliced
2 tablespoons sesame oil
2 teaspoons yellow mustard seeds
1 tablespoon light soy sauce
2 tablespoons freshly squeezed lime juice
pepper

1 Cut the carrot and celeriac into thin julienne strips or grate them coarsely by hand. Place in a bowl with the spring onions.
2 Heat the oil gently in a small frying pan. Add the mustard seeds. When they start to pop, remove the pan from the heat and add the seeds to the carrot and celeriac – be careful not to burn the mustard seeds or they will become bitter.
3 Mix the soy sauce and lime juice in a small bowl, add plenty of pepper and pour over the salad. Toss well and serve.

Serves 4–6
Preparation time: 10–15 minutes

Cucumber, Radish and Dill Salad

- 2 cucumbers
- 6 tablespoons sea salt
- 1 bunch of radishes, trimmed and thinly sliced
- 1 egg yolk
- 1 tablespoon coarse grain mustard
- 1 tablespoon clear honey
- 2 tablespoons lemon juice
- 3 tablespoons olive oil
- 3 tablespoons chopped fresh dill
- pepper

1 Cut both the cucumbers in half lengthways, scoop out the seeds if bitter, then slice the cucumbers very thinly crossways.

2 Layer the cucumber slices in a colander and sprinkle with the salt. Set the colander over a plate, or in the sink, to catch the juices and leave for 1–1½ hours. Rinse well under cold water, drain and pat the slices dry with a clean tea towel. Place in a salad bowl and add the radishes.

3 Place the egg yolk in a bowl with the mustard, honey and lemon juice. Whisk well to combine. Continue to whisk while gradually adding the oil in a thin stream until it is well amalgamated. Stir in the chopped dill. Add to the cucumber and radishes, toss well and serve.

Serves 4–6
Preparation time: 15 minutes, plus salting the cucumbers

Watercress and Pomegranate Salad

This is a beautiful and unusual salad, perfumed with fragrant rosewater and strewn with pomegranate seeds and orange segments. It is a stunning accompaniment to barbecued meat and game. Some people are allergic to pink peppercorns, so you may wish to omit them or substitute green peppercorns instead.

- 1 pomegranate
- 1 bunch of watercress, broken into sprigs
- 4 oranges
- 1 teaspoon rosewater
- 5 tablespoons olive oil
- 1 tablespoon raspberry vinegar
- 1 teaspoon bottled pink peppercorns in brine, drained (see left)
- sea salt flakes

1 Break open the pomegranate and remove the seeds, discarding the bitter yellow pith. Place the seeds in a large bowl with the watercress.

2 Finely grate the rind from 2 of the oranges and set aside. Peel and segment all the oranges, removing all the pith. Work over the bowl with the pomegranate and watercress to catch any juices.

3 In a separate bowl, combine the rosewater, olive oil, raspberry vinegar, pink peppercorns and the reserved grated orange rind. Mix well, pour over the watercress and pomegranate salad, season with a few sea salt flakes and serve.

Serves 4
Preparation time: 15 minutes

Baby Corn, Spring Onion and Coriander Salad

Crunchy little corn cobs in a dressing of spring onion, coriander and soy sauce make a memorable salad.

- 500 g/1 lb baby corn cobs, trimmed
- 2 tablespoons sesame seeds
- 6 spring onions, finely sliced
- 50 g/2 oz fresh coriander, chopped
- 50 ml/2 fl oz sunflower oil
- 2 teaspoons sesame oil
- 2 tablespoons freshly squeezed lime or lemon juice
- 1 tablespoon soy sauce
- 1–2 red chillies, deseeded and finely chopped (optional)
- salt and pepper

1 Bring a large saucepan of lightly salted water to the boil, add the corn and cook for 3–4 minutes until just tender. Drain in a colander, refresh under cold water and drain again well.
2 Place the sesame seeds in a dry frying pan. Heat, tossing, for 1–2 minutes, until evenly browned. Remove from the heat and set aside.
3 Mix the rest of the ingredients in a salad bowl, add the corn cobs and toss lightly. Sprinkle with the toasted sesame seeds and serve with slices of crusty bread.

Serves 4–6
Preparation time: 20 minutes
Cooking time: 3–4 minutes

Kohlrabi and Bean Sprout Salad

A fresh, crisp salad of crunchy bean sprouts and kohlrabi – a vegetable with a sweet, nutty flavour, sometimes called the cabbage-turnip.

- 75 g/3 oz unsalted cashew nuts
- 75 g/3 oz grated fresh coconut or 50 g/2 oz unsweetened desiccated coconut
- 250 g/8 oz kohlrabi
- 125 g/4 oz fresh bean sprouts, rinsed and dried
- 3 spring onions, finely chopped
- 1 tablespoon chopped fresh mint
- 1 garlic clove, crushed
- 2 tablespoons freshly squeezed lime juice
- 2 tablespoons clear honey

1 Scatter the cashew nuts on a baking sheet. Place in a preheated oven, 180°C (350°F), Gas Mark 4, for 10–15 minutes until evenly golden. Leave to cool, then chop coarsely.
2 If using desiccated coconut, place in a bowl with warm water to cover. Leave to soak for 20 minutes, then strain through a sieve, pressing the coconut against the sides with the back of a spoon to squeeze out any excess moisture.
3 Peel the kohlrabi and grate it coarsely into a bowl. Add the bean sprouts, coconut, spring onions and mint. Mix well.
4 Combine the garlic, lime juice and honey in a jug. Mix thoroughly and pour over the salad. Toss lightly, then sprinkle with the toasted cashew nuts.

Serves 4–6
Preparation time: 20 minutes
Cooking time: 10–15 minutes
Oven temperature: 180°C (350°F), Gas Mark 4

Celery and Fennel Salad with Blue Cheese Dressing

Fennel, with its light aniseed flavour, is delicious combined with celery, pears and pecan nuts in this salad.

- **3 spring onions, finely sliced**
- **75 g/3 oz pecans, finely chopped**
- **2 pears**
- **½ tablespoon lemon juice**
- **1 fennel bulb, trimmed and finely sliced**
- **4 celery sticks, finely sliced**

- **pepper**
- **escarole lettuce and watercress, to serve**

BLUE CHEESE DRESSING:
- **75 g/3 oz Roquefort or Gorgonzola cheese**
- **50 g/2 oz crème fraîche or soured cream**
- **1 tablespoon red wine vinegar**

1 First make the blue cheese dressing. Place the blue cheese, crème fraîche or soured cream and vinegar in a liquidizer or food processor or blender and purée until smooth. Alternatively, mix in a bowl and mash with a fork. Stir in the spring onions and 50 g/ 2 oz of the pecans.

2 Slice the pears in half and remove the cores. Cut the flesh into cubes, place in a bowl and mix with the lemon juice. Add the sliced fennel and celery to the pears.

3 To serve, arrange the salad leaves on individual serving plates or bowls. Top with the fennel, celery and pear mixture, spoon over the blue cheese dressing and sprinkle with the remaining pecans.

Serves 4–6
Preparation time: 20 minutes

Puy Lentil and Red Pepper Salad

- 375 g/12 oz dried puy lentils
- 1.2 litres/2 pints cold water
- 1 small onion, studded with 2 cloves
- 2 bay leaves
- 3 red peppers
- 1½ teaspoons coriander seeds, crushed
- 5 tablespoons olive oil
- 2–3 tablespoons lemon juice
- 2 garlic cloves, crushed
- salt and pepper

1 Place the lentils in a large saucepan with the water, the studded onion and the bay leaves. Bring to a boil and boil for 10 minutes, reduce the heat, cover and simmer gently for 15 minutes until the lentils are just tender. Drain well and remove the onion and bay leaves.

2 Place the peppers on a baking sheet under a preheated grill and leave to cook for 10–12 minutes, turning every now and then until blistered and well charred. Remove from the heat and place in a plastic bag, leave to cool then peel, deseed and cut into strips.

3 Mix together the coriander seeds, olive oil, lemon juice and garlic and add the drained lentils and red pepper strips. Toss together well, season to taste and serve.

Serves 6–8
Preparation time: 10 minutes
Cooking time: 35–40 minutes

Hot Potato Salad with Feta and Caper Vinaigrette

- 750 g/1½ lb small red skinned potatoes
- 125 g/4 oz feta cheese, crumbled

CAPER VINAIGRETTE:

- 1 tablespoon sherry vinegar
- ½ tablespoon Dijon mustard
- 2 tablespoons capers, drained and roughly chopped
- 1 tablespoon chopped tarragon
- 6 tablespoons extra virgin olive oil
- salt and pepper

1 Place the potatoes in a pan of lightly salted boiling water and cook for 10–15 minutes until just tender. Drain. Cut the potatoes in half if large.
2 To make the caper vinaigrette, mix together the vinegar, mustard, capers and tarragon. Gradually whisk in the olive oil in a steady stream until amalgamated and season with salt and pepper.
3 Toss the warm potatoes with the vinaigrette and sprinkle with the feta.

Serves 4
Preparation time: 10 minutes
Cooking time: 15 minutes

Couscous and Celery Salad

- **250 g/8 oz quick-cooking couscous**
- **6 celery sticks, very finely sliced**
- **1 red onion, finely sliced**
- **5 tablespoons chopped fresh mint**
- **5 tablespoons chopped fresh parsley**
- **2 teaspoons fennel seeds, crushed**
- **2 tablespoons olive oil**
- **finely grated rind and juice of 2 lemons**
- **salt and pepper**

1 Place the couscous in a bowl, add enough cold water to cover, then leave to stand for 30 minutes, until all the water has been absorbed.

2 Line a colander with muslin or a clean tea towel. Drain the couscous into the colander, then gather up the sides of the piece of muslin or the tea towel and squeeeze to extract as much of the liquid as possible from the couscous. Tip the couscous into a salad bowl.

3 Stir in the celery, onion, mint, parsley, fennel seeds, olive oil, lemon rind and half of the lemon juice. Add salt and pepper to taste. Cover and set aside for 30 minutes, then taste the salad and add more lemon juice if required.

Serves 6
Preparation time: 35 minutes, plus soaking

Orecchiette, Broad Bean and Pecorino Salad

'Orecchiette', meaning 'little ears', are pasta shapes with a soft creamy texture and go very well with this mixture of sharp Pecorino cheese and sweet baby broad beans. If you cannot find orecchiette, other similar short pasta shapes such as 'ruoti' or 'wheels' may be used instead.

- 750 g/1½ lb fresh young broad beans in the pod or 250 g/8 oz frozen broad beans, thawed
- 5 tablespoons extra virgin olive oil
- 500 g/1 lb orecchiette
- 75 g/3 oz Pecorino cheese, grated
- 50 g/2 oz pitted black olives, finely chopped
- 5 tablespoons chopped fresh flat leaf parsley
- 1 tablespoon balsamic vinegar
- salt and pepper

1 Shell the broad beans, if fresh. Bring a saucepan of lightly salted water to the boil, add the fresh or thawed frozen beans and blanch for 1 minute. Drain, refresh under cold water, then drain again. Pop the beans out of their skins.

2 Bring a large saucepan of boiling water to the boil with a little oil and salt, drop in the pasta and cook for 12–15 minutes until just tender. Drain the pasta in a colander, refresh under cold water and drain thoroughly again.

3 Tip the pasta into a large salad bowl and add the remaining ingredients. To serve, toss well and add a generous grinding of pepper.

Serves 4
Preparation time: 20 minutes

Red Pepper and Chickpea Salad

- 175 g/6 oz dried chickpeas, soaked
  overnight and drained
- 3 red peppers
- 12 black olives, pitted
- 2 tablespoons chopped fresh coriander

ORANGE DRESSING:

- 3 tablespoons sunflower oil
- ½ teaspoon grated orange rind
- 2 tablespoons orange juice
- 1 garlic clove, crushed
- salt and pepper

1 Cook the chickpeas in unsalted boiling water for 2 hours or until they are tender.

2 Meanwhile, place the red peppers under a hot grill for 15 minutes, turning them frequently, until the skins blacken and blister. Hold the peppers under cold water then, using a small sharp knife, peel off the skins. Cut the peppers in half, discard the cores and seeds, and slice the peppers.

3 To make the orange dressing, mix together the sunflower oil, orange rind and juice and garlic in a large bowl. Season to taste with salt and pepper.

4 Drain the chickpeas and toss in the orange dressing while they are still hot. Set aside to cool.

5 Stir in the red peppers, olives and fresh coriander. Turn the salad into a serving dish.

Serves 4
Preparation time: 10 minutes
Cooking time: 2 hours

Dessert Dishes

Grilled Fruit Skewers with Coconut Custard

1 kg/2 lb assorted fruits in season (e.g. mango, papaya, peach, strawberries, oranges, apples or pears)

lime or lemon juice, for brushing

2 tablespoons muscovado or caster sugar

COCONUT CUSTARD:

4 egg yolks

75 g/3 oz caster sugar

150 ml/¼ pint coconut milk

150 ml/¼ pint double cream

1 tablespoon rum, Cointreau or other liqueur (optional)

1 First make the coconut custard. Whisk the egg yolks and sugar in a bowl until thick and creamy. Mix the coconut milk and cream in a saucepan and bring to just below boiling point, then pour into the beaten egg yolk mixture, whisking constantly, then return to a clean pan. Place over low heat and stir constantly until the mixture coats the back of a spoon. Be careful not to let the mixture boil or the custard will curdle. Remove the pan from the heat and immediately strain the custard into a bowl. Stir in the rum or liqueur, if using, and cover closely. When cool, chill the custard in the refrigerator. If using wooden skewers, soak them in cold water for 30 minutes.

2 Prepare the fruit and cut it into even-sized pieces. Thread on to 8 skewers, alternating the different types, to create a colourful effect. Brush with lime or lemon juice. Cook on a barbecue grill over moderately hot coals for 2–3 minutes on each side, then sprinkle the fruit with the sugar and cook the skewers for 1 minute more. Serve at once, with a separate bowl of coconut custard for dipping, like a cold fondue.

Serves 4

Preparation time: 25 minutes, plus chilling

Cooking time: 4–6 minutes

Kissel of Summer Berries with Almond Bread Crisps

- 1 loaf almond bread (see right)
- 500 g/1 lb mixed summer berries (raspberries, strawberries, cherries and red, white or blackcurrants), prepared
- 600 ml/1 pint water
- 1 tablespoon arrowroot mixed to a paste with 2 tablespoons water (optional)
- 3–4 tablespoons sugar
- soured cream or fromage blanc, to serve (optional)

1 To make the almond bread crisps, cut the loaf into very thin slices and arrange in a single layer on a baking sheet. Bake in a preheated oven, 150°C (300°F) Gas Mark 2, for 15–20 minutes until lightly golden. Cool on wire racks. Store in an airtight container.
2 To make the kissel, set aside 125 g/4 oz of the fruit for decoration. Place the remaining fruit with the measured water in a saucepan. Bring to the boil, then turn off the heat and leave to cool slightly. Pour into a food processor or blender, work until smooth, then strain through a sieve into a clean saucepan to remove any pips or seeds.
3 Bring the purée to the boil. Whisk in the arrowroot paste , if using, with the sugar. When the purée thickens, pour it into a bowl and cover closely to prevent a skin forming. Cool, then chill.
4 Pour the chilled kissel into soup plates and decorate with the reserved fruit. Swirl in the soured cream or fromage blanc, if using, and serve the almond bread crisps separately.

Serves 6
Preparation time: 15 minutes
Cooking time: 15–20 minutes

Almond Bread

- 2 eggs
- 125 g/4 oz caster sugar
- ½ teaspoon vanilla essence
- 125 g/4 oz plain flour, sifted
- 125 g/4 oz whole blanched almonds, toasted

1 Grease a 20 x 7 cm/8 x 3 inch loaf tin and line it with nonstick baking paper.
2 Whisk the eggs, sugar and vanilla essence in a bowl until thick and creamy and the mixture holds a trail when the whisk is lifted.Carefully fold in the flour and almonds and spoon into the loaf tin. Level the top.
3 Bake in a preheated oven, 160°C (325°F), Gas Mark 3, for 30–35 minutes or until a skewer comes out clean. Cool slightly in the tin, then invert on to a rack to cool completely.

Serves 6
Preparation time: 15 minutes
Cooking time: 30–35 minutes
Oven temperature: 160°C (325°F), Gas Mark 3

Apricot Clafoutis

A slightly different version of the classic French dessert (usually made with cherries) made here with fresh apricots in a sweetened batter.

- 750 g/1½ lb fresh apricots
- 4 eggs, beaten
- 125 g/4 oz caster sugar, plus extra for sprinkling
- pinch of salt
- 50 g/2 oz plain flour
- 250 ml/8 fl oz milk
- 50 g/2 oz butter
- 2 tablespoons apricot brandy
- crème fraîche, to serve

1 Grease a 28 x18 cm/11 x 7 inch shallow ovenproof dish. Cut the apricots in half, remove the stones and place cut side up in the dish.

2 Whisk the eggs, sugar and salt in a bowl. Whisk in the flour, beat until smooth and finally whisk in the milk until well combined. Melt 25 g/1oz of the butter and beat into the batter mixture with the apricot brandy.

3 Pour the batter over the apricots in the dish and dot with the remaining butter. Place in a preheated oven, 200°C (400°F), Gas Mark 6, for 35–40 minutes until the batter is golden and just set and the fruit is tender. Sprinkle with sugar and serve with crème fraîche.

Serves 4–6

Preparation time: 15 minutes
Cooking time: 35-40 minutes
Oven temperature: 200°C (400°F), Gas Mark 6

VARIATION

Peach Clafoutis

Replace the apricots with 750 g/1½ lb peaches, stones removed and the flesh quartered. Substitute crème de pêche or another liqueur of your choice for the apricot brandy.

Baked Bananas with Cinnamon and Rum Mascarpone Cream

Freshly baked bananas are sold at small roadside stalls in Thailand. Hot and deliciously sweet, with just a squeeze of fresh lime juice, they must be just about the best fast food ever invented! In this version they are served with a mouthwatering mascarpone cream flavoured with cinnamon and rum.

- 1–2 tablespoons caster sugar
- ½ teaspoon ground cinnamon
- 2 teaspoons rum
- 250 g/8 oz mascarpone
- 8 small bananas

1 Mix the sugar, cinnamon and rum in a bowl. Stir in the mascarpone, mix well and set aside.

2 Place the whole unpeeled bananas on a barbecue grill over hot coals and cook for 10–12 minutes, turning the bananas as the skins darken, until they are black all over and the flesh is very tender.

3 To serve, split the bananas open and spread the flesh with the cinnamon and rum mascarpone cream.

Serves 4
Preparation: time: 5 minutes
Cooking time: 10–12 minutes

VARIATION

Baked Bananas with Chocolate Ricotta Cream

- 250 g/8 oz ricotta
- 1–2 tablespoons maple syrup
- 25 g/1 oz chopped roasted hazelnuts
- 50 g/2 oz dark chocolate, melted

1 Mix the ricotta and maple syrup in a bowl. Stir in half of the hazelnuts and beat in the melted chocolate.

2 Prepare the baked bananas as in the main recipe and serve with the chocolate ricotta cream. Sprinkle with the remaining hazelnuts.

Baked Blueberry Purses with Almond Cream

Plain sugar can be substituted for the vanilla sugar, but the latter is very easy to prepare at home. Just place one or two vanilla pods in a jar of sugar for a few days. They will scent the sugar deliciously, and you can top up the jar with more sugar as and when required. It is not essential to drain the mascarpone cheese overnight but this will remove any excess moisture and firm up the mixture.

- 750 g/1½ lb fresh blueberries
- 6 tablespoons vanilla sugar (see introduction)
- 6 tablespoons crème de cassis

ALMOND CREAM:
- 750g/1½ lb ground almonds
- 1 kg/2 lb mascarpone
- 3 egg yolks
- 125 g/4 oz caster sugar
- 125 ml/4 fl oz double cream
- 2 tablespoons Amaretto

1 To make the almond cream, first line an 18 cm/7 inch sieve with a piece of muslin large enough to overhang the edge by about 10 cm/4 inches. Place the sieve over a bowl.
2 In a mixing bowl, beat the ground almonds with the mascarpone. In a separate bowl, beat the egg yolks with the sugar until they are pale and fluffy. Fold into the mascarpone mixture.

3 Whip the cream in another bowl until it forms soft peaks. Fold into the mascarpone with the Amaretto. Turn the mixture into the lined sieve, fold the excess muslin over, cover with a small plate and set a small weight on top. Place in the refrigerator for 6–8 hours or overnight, to drain.
4 The blueberries are cooked in individual foil purses. For each purse you will require a 33 x 33 cm/13 x 13 inch square of double foil. Heap a quarter of the blueberries in the centre of each foil square and turn up the edges of the foil to form a lip. Sprinkle the blueberries with 1 tablespoon of

vanilla sugar. Drizzle 1 tablespoon crème de cassis over the top, bring up the edges of the foil to make a purse and press together to seal.
5 Cook the sealed foil purses on a barbecue grill over moderately hot coals for 8–10 minutes.
6 Unmould the almond cream on to a large plate. Serve portions of the cream beside the blueberries and a jug of single cream, if liked.

Serves 6–8
Preparation: time: 15 minutes, plus draining overnight
Cooking time: 10 minutes

Melon and Rosewater Granita

A fresh icy granita is perfect as a light dessert after a rich main dish, or served between courses to clear the palate. Although is takes time, it is very easy to make.

- 2 Charentais or rock melons
- 75 g/3 oz caster sugar
- 175 ml/6 fl oz water
- ½ teaspoon rosewater
- fromage frais, to serve (optional)

1 Cut the melons in half, remove the seeds and scoop out the flesh into a food processor or blender.
2 Place the sugar and measured water in a saucepan and heat for about 1–2 minutes until the sugar has dissolved. Increase the heat and boil for another 2 minutes without stirring, then remove from heat and leave to cool slightly.
3 Add half of the sugar syrup to the melon flesh and blend until smooth. Pour into a bowl and stir in the rosewater and more sugar syrup to taste; the amount needed will depend on the sweetness of the fruit.
4 Pour the melon mixture into a 25 x 15 cm/10 x 6 inch tin and chill in the refrigerator. When the mixture is quite cold, transfer the tin to the freezer for 1 hour or until ice crystals have formed around the rim and the mixture is starting to freeze on the base. Stir the mixture thoroughly with a fork, then replace in the freezer. Repeat every 45 minutes until uniform crystals have formed. This will take approximately 4–5 hours. Serve at once or within 4–6 hours. To serve, spoon into glasses and top with a dollop of fromage frais, if liked.

Serves 4–6
Preparation time: 10 minutes, plus freezing
Cooking time: about 5 minutes

VARIATION

Orange Granita

Place 250 g/8 oz granulated sugar in a saucepan with 600 ml/1 pint water over moderate heat and stir until dissolved. Bring to the boil and boil for 5 minutes. Let the syrup cool to room temperature, then stir in 350 ml/ 12 fl oz unsweetened orange juice, 2 tablespoons of lemon juice and 1 teaspoon of finely grated orange rind. Pour into shallow freezerproof tray and freeze until the mixture has a snowy, granular texture, stirring every 30 minutes. Serve as for the main recipe.

Grilled Honeyed Peaches

Sweet fragrant peaches served hot from the grill with a Marsala flavoured syrup and crunchy amaretti biscuits make a a simple but spectacular dessert. Use very ripe peaches as they have the best flavour.

- 4 ripe peaches
- 300 ml/½ pint Marsala
- 4 tablespoons honey
- 1 strip of orange rind
- 25 g/1 oz butter, melted
- 4 amaretti biscuits
- vanilla ice cream or crème fraîche, to serve

1 Cut a small cross in the top and bottom of each peach and place it in a pan of boiling water, leave for 20 seconds and transfer with a slotted spoon to a bowl of cold water. Peel, cut in half lengthways and remove the stone.

2 Place the Marsala, honey and orange rind in a small saucepan, bring to the boil, then simmer for 2 minutes. Add the peach halves and simmer for 3–4 minutes until just tender. Remove the pan from the heat and leave the peaches to cool in the syrup.

3 Remove the peaches with a slotted spoon and place the remaining syrup in a small pan. Bring to the boil and reduce by half.

4 Brush the peaches with the melted butter and place on the preheated barbecue for 5–7 minutes, turning once.

5 Transfer the hot peaches to serving plates, spoon over a 1ittle of the reduced syrup and crumble over the amaretti biscuits. Serve with vanilla ice cream or crème fraîche.

Serves 4
Preparation time : 15 minutes
Cooking time : 5–7 minutes

Champagne Syllabub and Strawberries

What evokes the taste of summer more than perfectly ripened, sweet English strawberries and cream? Here they are served with a velvety Champagne syllabub, ideal for a light but wicked dessert.

- 150 ml/¼ pint Champagne or sparkling dry white wine
- 2 tablespoons caster sugar
- finely grated rind and juice of ½ lemon
- 300 ml/½ pint double cream
- ripe strawberries, to serve

1 Mix together the Champagne, sugar, lemon rind and juice in a large bowl. Add the cream and whisk the mixture until it holds soft peaks. Spoon into glasses, then chill in the refrigerator for 1–2 hours before serving.
2 Serve with a mixture of cultivated and wild strawberries.

Serves 4
Preparation time: 5–10 minutes, plus chilling

Chestnut Flan with Persimmon Cream Pots

Perfect for autumn – slices of chestnut flan with puréed fruit and cream piled into frozen persimmon shells. The fruit must be very soft and ripe – unripe persimmons have very dry, tannic and unpleasant taste.

- 500 g/1 lb cooked chestnuts, peeled
- 125 g/4 oz butter, softened
- 200 g/7 oz caster sugar
- ½ teaspoon vanilla essence
- 2 eggs, separated, plus 1 egg white
- 1 teaspoon fennel seeds, crushed (optional)
- icing sugar, for dusting

PERSIMMON POTS:
- 6 ripe persimmons
- 350 ml/12 fl oz double cream
- 3 tablespoons caster sugar
- grated nutmeg

1 First prepare the persimmon pots. Cut a 5 mm/¼ inch slice off the top of each fruit, making a lid. Using a teaspoon, scoop the persimmon flesh into a sieve set over a bowl, leaving a thin shell. Wrap all the persimmon shells and lids in clingfilm and freeze for 1–2 hours until firm. Meanwhile, press the persimmon flesh through the sieve, discarding the stones.
2 Purée the chestnuts in a food processor or blender until smooth.
3 Beat the butter, sugar and vanilla essence until light and fluffy. Stir in the egg yolks, chestnut purée and fennel seeds, if using. Mix well.
4 Whisk the egg whites in a grease-free bowl until stiff but not dry. Stir a quarter into the chestnut mixture and gently fold in the rest. Spoon the mixture into a 20 cm/8 inch fluted flan tin. Level the surface. Bake in a preheated oven, 160°C (325°F) Gas Mark 3, for 40–50 minutes, until a skewer inserted in the flan comes out clean. Cool slightly, then transfer to a wire rack to cool completely .

5 Whisk the cream, sugar and nutmeg until it forms soft peaks. Fold in the persimmon purée, then spoon into the frozen shells and top with the lids. Dust the flan with the icing sugar and serve with the persimmon cream pots.

Serves 6–8
Preparation time: 20 minutes, plus freezing
Cooking time: 40–50 minutes
Oven temperature: 160°C (325°F) Gas Mark 3

Chocolate and Pine Nut Meringue Stack

- 50 g/2 oz cocoa powder
- 125 g/4 oz icing sugar
- 6 egg whites
- pinch of salt
- 175 g/6 oz caster sugar
- 125 g/4 oz pine nuts, toasted and chopped
- icing sugar and cocoa powder, to decorate

MARSALA CREAM:

- 2 eggs, separated
- 2 tablespoons caster sugar
- 2 tablespoons Marsala
- 500 g/1 lb mascarpone

1 Line 4 baking sheets with nonstick baking paper. Draw a 20 cm/8 inch circle on each one.
2 Sift the cocoa powder and icing sugar into a small bowl. Place the egg whites and salt in a separate, grease-free bowl and whisk until stiff but not dry. Gradually whisk in the caster sugar, 1 tablespoon at a time. Fold in the icing sugar mixture and chopped pine nuts until evenly combined.
3 Divide the meringue mixture evenly between the circles on the lined baking sheets and spread out evenly with a palette knife. Place the baking sheets in a preheated oven, 150°C (300°F), Gas Mark 2, and bake for 1–1½ hours. Remove from the oven and cool completely on wire racks.
4 To make the marsala cream, whisk the egg yolks, caster sugar and Marsala in a bowl until creamy, then beat in the mascarpone until well combined. Place the egg whites in a separate, greasefree bowl and whisk until stiff but not dry, then fold them into the mascarpone mixture.
5 Divide the marsala cream mixture among 3 of the meringue bases, spreading to the edges. Stack the cream-topped meringues on top of each other on a serving plate, then crush the last layer into small pieces and sprinkle on top. Place the dessert in the refrigerator for 2–4 hours. Serve lightly dusted with icing sugar and cocoa powder.

Serves 8–10
Preparation time: 35 minutes, plus chilling
Cooking time: 1–1½ hours
Oven temperature: 150°C (300°F), Gas Mark 2

Recipe Photographers:
Reed International Books Ltd.
/Gus Filgate /James Merrell
/Hilary Moore
Recipe Home Economist:
Annie Nichols
Jacket Photographer:
Gus Filgate
Jacket Home Economist:
Louise Pickford